Crystallization-Study
of the
Gospel
of Mark

Volume One

Witness Lee

The Holy Word for Morning Revival

Living Stream Ministry
Anaheim, CA • www.lsm.org

First Edition, January 2007.

ISBN 0-7363-3379-7

Published by

Living Stream Ministry
2431 W. La Palma Ave., Anaheim, CA 92801 U.S.A.
P. O. Box 2121, Anaheim, CA 92814 U.S.A.

Printed in the United States of America

07 08 09 10 11 12 13 / 10 9 8 7 6 5 4 3 2 1

Contents

Preface

1. This book is intended as an aid to believers in developing a daily time of morning revival with the Lord in His word. At the same time, it provides a limited review of the Winter Training on the "Crystallization-study of the Gospel of Mark" held in Anaheim, California, December 25-30, 2006. Through intimate contact with the Lord in His word, the believers can be constituted with life and truth and thereby equipped to prophesy in the meetings of the church unto the building up of the Body of Christ.

2. The entire content of this book is taken from the *Crystallization-study Outlines: The Gospel of Mark,* the text and footnotes of the Recovery Version of the Bible, selections from the writings of Witness Lee and Watchman Nee, and *Hymns,* all of which are published by Living Stream Ministry.

3. The book is divided into weeks. One training message is covered per week. Each week presents first the message outline, followed by six daily portions, a hymn, and then some space for writing. The training outline has been divided into days, corresponding to the six daily portions. Each daily portion covers certain points and begins with a section entitled "Morning Nourishment." This section contains selected verses and a short reading that can provide rich spiritual nourishment through intimate fellowship with the Lord. The "Morning Nourishment" is followed by a section entitled "Today's Reading," a longer portion of ministry related to the day's main points. Each day's portion concludes with a short list of references for further reading and some space for the saints to make notes concerning their spiritual inspiration, enlightenment, and enjoyment to serve as a reminder of what they have received of the Lord that day.

4. The space provided at the end of each week is for composing a short prophecy. This prophecy can be composed by considering all of our daily notes, the "harvest" of our inspirations during the week, and preparing a main point

with some sub-points to be spoken in the church meetings for the organic building up of the Body of Christ.

5. Following the last week in this volume, we have provided reading schedules for both the Old and New Testaments in the Recovery Version with footnotes. These schedules are arranged so that one can read through both the Old and New Testaments of the Recovery Version with footnotes in two years.

6. As a practical aid to the saints' feeding on the Word throughout the day, we have provided verse cards at the end of the volume, which correspond to each day's Scripture reading. These may be cut out and carried along as a source of spiritual enlightenment and nourishment in the saints' daily lives.

7. The *Crystallization-study Outlines* were compiled by Living Stream Ministry from the writings of Witness Lee and Watchman Nee. The outlines, footnotes, and references in the Recovery Version of the Bible are by Witness Lee. All of the other references cited in this publication are from the published ministry of Witness Lee and Watchman Nee.

Winter Training
(December 25-30, 2006)

CRYSTALLIZATION-STUDY
OF
THE GOSPEL OF MARK

Banners:

When we live in the mingled spirit,
we are learning Christ according to
the reality in Jesus by the Spirit of reality
so that His biography becomes our history
to be the reality of the Body of Christ.

The kingdom of God is the Lord Jesus
sown as a seed into the believers and
developing into a realm over which
God can rule in the divine life.

Christ's person with His all-inclusive death
and His wonderful resurrection
is our all-inclusive replacement
for the producing of the one new man,
so we must "hear Him" and see "Jesus only."

Let us go forth and preach Christ
to all the creation, proclaiming the gospel,
presenting the truth, and ministering life
for the growth, development, and manifestation
of the kingdom of God.

*Living in the Reality of the Body of Christ
according to the Bird's-eye View
of the Reality in Jesus in the Gospel of Mark*

Scripture Reading: Eph. 4:20-24; Mark 1:15, 35; 4:23-25; 8:22-26; 6:45-52; 9:7-9; 10:45; 16:7

Day 1 I. **The desire of God's heart is that the reality in Jesus, the God-man living of Jesus as recorded in the four Gospels, would be duplicated in the many members of Christ's Body by the Spirit of reality to become the reality of the Body of Christ, the highest peak in God's economy (Eph. 4:20-24, 3-4):**

A. The reality of the Body of Christ is the corporate living of the perfected God-men, who live the divine life of their new man by denying the natural life of their old man according to the model of Christ as the first God-man (Mark 8:34; Rom. 6:4-6; Gal. 2:20; Eph. 3:16-17a; 1 Pet. 2:21).

B. The reality of the Body of Christ is the Spirit of reality, who is the Spirit of Jesus, mingled with our spirit; the Spirit of Jesus includes the reality in Jesus, the God-man living of Jesus (John 16:13; Acts 16:7; Rom. 8:16; 1 Cor. 6:17).

C. When we live in the mingled spirit, we are learning Christ according to the reality in Jesus by the Spirit of reality according to His model as the Slave-Savior in the Gospel of Mark so that His biography becomes our history; the living of the Body of Christ as the new man should be exactly the same as the living of Jesus revealed in the Gospel of Mark (Gal. 6:17-18; Rom. 1:1, 9; Eph. 4:20-24; Phil. 2:5).

Day 2 II. **We need to live in the reality of the Body of Christ by entering into the reality of the Gospel of Mark through the Spirit of reality (John 16:13):**

A. The biography of Jesus in the Gospel of Mark is

also our biography, our history, with Peter as our representative (16:7; *Hymns,* #949, stanza 4):

1. In the angel's message to the three sisters who discovered the resurrection of the Slave-Savior, the phrase *and Peter* is inserted only in Mark's record (v. 7); the Gospel of Mark is considered to be a written account dictated by Peter and written down by his spiritual son, Mark (1 Pet. 5:13).

2. Even though Peter had committed the great sin of denying the Lord three times, the Lord specifically mentioned him; this is the gospel (Mark 14:67-72; Luke 15:1-7; John 21:15-17).

3. *And Peter* means "and you," who have failed like Peter, revealing that although we fail the Lord, it is impossible for Him to forget us, forsake us, give up on us, or not love us; if we fall, He will not desert us, and He can make us rise up again for His economy (Rom. 14:4, 7-8; Deut. 31:6; Josh. 1:5; Heb. 13:5; Isa. 49:14-16; Jer. 29:11-14; Prov. 24:16; cf. S. S. 8:6).

Day 3 B. Mark 6:45-52 reveals that we need to seek out the journey, the course, that the Lord has ordained for us according to His perfect will and to enjoy Him as our heavenly Minister and High Priest, the One who is interceding for us and sustaining us to finish our course in living a heavenly life on earth for the reality of the Body of Christ (Heb. 8:1-2; 7:26; Acts 20:24; 2 Tim. 4:7-8):

1. From the ascension of Christ to His coming again, the world is in a long night; "the night is far advanced" (Rom. 13:12), our boat is "in the midst of the sea," and we still have not reached the destination of our journey (Mark 6:45-48; John 6:21; cf. 2 Thes. 2:2; 2 Tim. 3:1-13).

2. We need to realize that the journey of faithful believers is one that is "contrary to the wind," and they experience being "distressed" as they "row"; we need to take the Lord into our "boat" (our married life, our family, our business, etc.) and enjoy peace with Him on the journey of human life (Mark 6:47-51; John 6:21).

3. In these days, just before the dawn of the Lord's coming (2 Pet. 1:19), we need to stand against the wearing-out tactics of Satan (Dan. 7:25), be empowered in the grace which is in Christ Jesus (2 Tim. 2:1), and receive mercy from the Lord to be faithful (1 Cor. 7:25b) to take the journey that He has ordained for the building up of His Body, His bride, to bring Him back (Matt. 16:18; Gen. 2:22; Rev. 19:7).

Day 4

C. In order to enter into the reality of the Gospel of Mark, we need to repent, to have a change of mind with regret for the past and a turn for the future; to repent is to turn from all things other than God to God Himself (Mark 1:15):

1. On the negative side, to repent before God is not only to repent of sins and wrongdoings but also to repent of the world and its corruption, which usurp and corrupt people whom God created for Himself, and to repent of our God-forsaking life in the past (Isa. 55:7; 2 Pet. 3:9-10, 15).

2. On the positive side, it is to turn to God in every way and in everything for the fulfillment of His purpose in creating man; it is a "repentance unto God," and is to "repent and turn to God" (Acts 20:21; 26:20).

3. Repentance unto life, unto God's organic salvation in life, is a gift given to us from the exalted Christ (5:31; 11:18).

4. Christ as the kindness of God leads us to

repentance so that, according to His mercy, we can be reconditioned, remade, and remodeled with Him as life (Rom. 2:4; Titus 3:4-5).

5. Repentance is a divine requirement of God's New Testament economy and a main item of its proclamation (Acts 17:30; Luke 24:47).

D. In order to enter into the reality of the Gospel of Mark, we need to "hear Him!" and see "Jesus only" (9:7-9; cf. Rev. 1:10, 12):

1. We need to take heed to the way we hear the word of the Lord, asking the Lord to give us an ear to hear what the Spirit is speaking to the churches; the measure that can be given to us by the Lord depends on the measure of our hearing (Mark 4:23-25; Rev. 2:7).

2. We need to have a private and intimate time with the Lord so that He can infuse us with His element to recover our sight; we all need a further recovery so that we can "see all things clearly" (Mark 8:22-26).

Day 5 III. **We need to live in the reality of the Body of Christ according to the bird's-eye view of the reality in Jesus in the Gospel of Mark, which unveils a full picture of the Slave-Savior serving fallen sinners as a collective person with Himself as their all-inclusive salvation; the life of the Lord Jesus as revealed in Mark is the reality, substance, and pattern of God's New Testament economy (1:35-38; 10:45):**

A. The Gospel of Mark shows the Slave-Savior coming as a Physician with mercy and grace to heal and recover a complete, sick person with four kinds of major diseases; just as God desires to show mercy to pitiful sinners, so He wants us to show mercy in love to others (2:17; 12:33; Matt. 9:12-13; Micah 6:6-8):

1. A fever may signify a person's unbridled temper, which is abnormal and intemperate;

the Slave-Savior heals our sick condition, becoming our inward rest and quietness, and restores us to normality that we might serve Him (Mark 1:29-31; Isa. 30:15a; cf. Prov. 15:1; 25:15).

2. Leprosy is the most contaminating and damaging disease, causing its victim to be isolated from God and from men; the cleansing of the leper signifies the recovering of the sinner to the fellowship with God and with men (Mark 1:40-45; Num. 12:1-10; 2 Kings 5:1, 9-14; Mark 14:3; 1 John 1:3).

3. The paralytic signifies a sinner who is paralyzed by sin, one who is unable to walk and move before God; through the forgiveness of our sins in Christ's judicial redemption, we are able to walk and move by the Spirit in God's organic salvation (Mark 2:1-12; 1 John 1:7, 9; Gal. 5:25).

4. The flow of blood, the issue of blood, signifies a life that cannot be retained; by touching the Lord, His divine power is transfused, through the perfection of His humanity, into us to become our healing; the God who dwells in unapproachable light became touchable in the Slave-Savior through His humanity for our salvation and enjoyment (Mark 5:25-34).

B. After the healing of the entire person, there is the Lord's exposure and cleansing of the real inner being, the heart (7:1-23).

C. In addition to this healing, there are three feedings by the Lord—the feeding of five thousand (6:30-44), the feeding of the Gentiles as the pet dogs under the table (7:27), and the feeding of four thousand (8:1-9).

D. After this collective person is healed, cleansed within, and fed by the Lord, he needs the specific healing of his listening organ, speaking organ, and seeing organ (7:31-37; 8:14-26).

E. Now on the Mount of Transfiguration, his ears are opened to hear the Lord Jesus as the Father's Son, the Beloved, and his eyes are opened to see "Jesus only," to see that He is the unique and universal replacement to be the unique constituent of the one new man (8:27—9:13; Col. 3:10-11).

Day 6

F. The Lord then brings His followers as a collective person into His all-inclusive death (Mark 15:16-41) and His all-surpassing resurrection (16:1-18) so that they may enjoy Him in His all-transcending ascension (v. 19) as their life and life supply (John 6:35, 57), the Lord of all (Acts 10:36), God's Christ (2:36), the Head over all things to the church (Eph. 1:22-23a), the Head of the Body (Col. 1:18), the glorified One (Luke 24:26), the enthroned One (Acts 5:31), the One who is above all (Eph. 1:20-21), and the One who fills all in all (v. 23b) to bring forth the new man as the reality of the kingdom of God (Col. 3:10-11; Rom. 14:17), consummating in the New Jerusalem (Rev. 21:2).

G. Finally, the Lord as the resurrected and ascended Slave-Savior preaches the gospel through His disciples as His reproduction for His universal spreading, until He comes again to set up the kingdom of God on earth (Mark 16:20; Luke 19:12; Dan. 7:13-14; Matt. 24:14).

Morning Nourishment

Eph. 4:22-24 That you put off, as regards your former manner of life, the old man, which is being corrupted,...and *that* you be renewed in the spirit of your mind and put on the new man, which was created according to God...

Mark 8:34 ...He called the crowd to *Him* with His disciples and said to them, If anyone wants to follow after Me, let him deny himself and take up his cross and follow Me.

1 Pet. 2:21 For to this you were called, because Christ also suffered on your behalf, leaving you a model so that you may follow in His steps.

We are being discipled from being a natural man to being a God-man, living the divine life by denying our natural life according to the model of Christ as the first God-man (Matt. 28:19).

When Christ was on this earth, He denied His natural life, Himself. He said that whatever He spoke was not His word but the word of the Father who sent Him (John 14:24). He never did anything out of Himself (5:19, 30). He did everything out of and by the sending Father. He was not the Sender but the Sent One. He did not live Himself; instead, He lived the Sender, the Father (6:57a). This is the model of the first God-man. (*The Vital Groups*, p. 36)

Today's Reading

When the Lord Jesus lived on the earth, He was genuinely a man, but instead of living by the life of man He lived by God as His life. Thus, in His life and in His living He lived the divine attributes as His human virtues manifested before the eyes of men. When people looked at Him, outwardly they saw that He was really a man. However, the more they observed Him and the more they followed Him, the more they had to admit that He truly was God....In the beginning they realized that He was the son of a carpenter, that He was a man. Gradually, the more they observed Him, the more they saw the virtues that were manifested in the Lord Jesus. Those virtues could never have been something of man....Those virtues were lived out of the God-man Jesus, who as a man lived not by Himself but by God and who lived out the divine attributes and manifested them as the virtues of such a One who is God yet man.

After the Lord practically lived out a typical God-man, He accomplished redemption through His death and resurrection to redeem us and regenerate us to be the same as He is. We are of the same life and nature as He. In this way we become God and we become the children of God. However, we still have many negative things in us. Thank the Lord,...He went to the cross with our flesh and with our sinful human nature. We all were dealt with by Him on the cross. Our old man has been crucified with Him; thus, the old creation, the flesh, Satan, and the world, that is, everything involved with the old man, were also dealt with on the cross. Today, since we have been regenerated, we should no longer participate in or live by these things. Rather, we should reject our self as the Lord Jesus denied His self. Our self is corrupt, even corrupt to the extent of being incurable. Christ has not one bit of evil in Him and He is absolutely good, yet He had to put aside His good self. This being the case, how much more do we need to put aside our evil self.

The Christian life which the Lord desires is one in which we are all day long, every minute and every second, under death, having one life and one living with the indwelling Triune God, the pneumatic Christ, the life-giving Spirit.

The reality of the Body of Christ is the union and mingling of God with man to live out a corporate God-man. For this we need to pass through death and resurrection, dying daily and being resurrected daily. We also need to be in the Spirit and walk according to the Spirit daily.

The way to live out the reality of the Body of Christ is to go through death and resurrection by the living together of God with man. (*The High Peak of the Vision and the Reality of the Body of Christ,* pp. 48-52, 54-55)

Further Reading: The High Peak of the Vision and the Reality of the Body of Christ, chs. 3-4; A Thorough View of the Body of Christ, chs. 2-3

Enlightenment and inspiration: _____

_____

_____

_____

Morning Nourishment

Mark **But go, tell His disciples and Peter that He is going**
16:7 **before you into Galilee. There you will see Him, even**
as He told you.

This wonderful One, who is the embodiment of the Father, and
whose realization is the Spirit, is the constituent of the church.
Our living through Him, with Him, by Him, and in Him is the
constitution of the practical church life....The church as the new
man is constituted with Christ as the inner constituent. Christ is
every member of the new man and is within every member. In the
new man Christ is all and in all (Col. 3:10-11). This is not only His
history but also our story. His biography becomes our history.

In the first chapter of Genesis, God made man in His image,
who is Christ, the image of the invisible God (Col. 1:15). In the last
chapter of Revelation, Christ is "the Spirit." Revelation 22:17
speaks of "the Spirit and the bride." The conclusion of the holy
Word reveals that the organic Triune God becomes fully mingled
with us, the transformed, tripartite human beings. His name at
the consummation of the divine revelation is "the Spirit."...He
has become "the Spirit" mingled with us, the transformed, tripartite man as His bride. He as the Husband and we as the bride
become a universal couple. This couple is the coming New Jerusalem, and this will be the history, the story, the biography of Him
with us for eternity. This biography began in eternity past and
lasts without end through eternity future. In between eternity
past and future, we are regenerated, renewed, sanctified, transformed, conformed, and glorified. We are in the process, in the
way and on the way, of the biography of this wonderful One. (*Five*
Emphases in the Lord's Recovery, pp. 27-28)

Today's Reading

[In the Gospel of Mark, Peter is our representative.] Peter was
the first to be called by the Lord. After he was called, he was
always taking the lead. He even took the lead to deny the Lord
Jesus. We may even say that, in a sense, Peter was crucified
before the Lord Jesus was. Then after the Lord's resurrection

Peter's name was mentioned by the angel: "But go, tell His disciples and Peter that He is going before you into Galilee" (16:7).

When we study the Gospel of Mark, we are actually studying our own biography. This means that the biography of Jesus is also our biography. In the words of a hymn, "He is my history," and "His life is my experience" (*Hymns*, #949). Therefore, the biography narrated in Mark is not only a biography of the individual Jesus but also a biography of the believers.

In particular, the Gospel of Mark is a biography of Peter, our representative. Peter is present in the first chapter of Mark, and his name is specifically mentioned in the last chapter…(16:7). Furthermore, the cases in this book are a composite portrait of us as represented by Peter. For example, on the Mount of Transfiguration Peter said, "Rabbi, it is good for us to be here; and let us make three tents, one for You and one for Moses and one for Elijah" (9:5). Because Peter is our representative, his speaking here is also our speaking. Likewise, when Peter denied the Lord three times, that was also our threefold denial of the Lord. The angel's word concerning Peter in 16:7 is also a word concerning us.

From the time Peter was called by the Lord Jesus in 1:16 and 17, he was captured by Him and was always with Him. Along with James and John, he was with the Lord on the Mount of Transfiguration. This indicates that wherever the Lord Jesus went, Peter went with Him, for the Lord brought Peter with Him.

Do you believe that when the Lord Jesus was crucified, He left Peter and the other disciples? No, when the Lord Jesus was crucified and buried, Peter, the representative of us all, was crucified with Him. Moreover, the Lord Jesus was not resurrected alone. According to God's point of view, which is beyond the elements of space and time, we all were included in Christ's resurrection. (*Life-study of Mark*, pp. 503, 519-20)

Further Reading: Five Emphases in the Lord's Recovery, ch. 2; *Life-study of Mark*, msgs. 59, 61; *The Collected Works of Watchman Nee*, vol. 18, pp. 251-254

Enlightenment and inspiration: _____

_____

_____

_____

Morning Nourishment

Mark   And immediately He compelled His disciples to step
6:45-48   into the boat and go before to the other side....And...
He went away to the mountain to pray. And when
evening fell,...He was alone on the land. And seeing
them distressed as they rowed, for the wind was
contrary to them, He came toward them about the
fourth watch of the night, walking on the sea...
51   And He went up unto them into the boat, and the
wind ceased....

[Mark 6:30-56 speaks of the Lord Jesus feeding five thousand
with five loaves and two fish (vv. 30-44), walking on the sea (vv. 45-
52), and healing many who were sick (vv. 53-56).] These three
events form a large type prefiguring the time of the Lord Jesus'
death on the cross to the time of His establishing the kingdom.
They tell us how the Lord: (1) was crucified for us, (2) ascended to
the heaven to become the High Priest for our sake, and (3) will
descend again in the future to establish the kingdom.

The account [in Mark 6] of the Lord compelling the disciples
to journey across the sea...was inserted between the cross and
the kingdom. This is an event for today, an event for the church
age....The Lord has died for them and is now constraining them
to take the journey. The Lord has one journey for His disciples,
and He constrained them to take it. The most important thing in
the Christian life is to seek out the journey which the Lord has
ordained and faithfully walk on it....The most important task
for each of us is to put ourselves into God's hand in a quiet,
patient, prayerful, consecrated, and obedient way and whole-
heartedly seek after His leading. (*The Collected Works of Watchman Nee*, vol. 10, pp. 424, 423)

Today's Reading

Mark 6:46...indicates to us how our Lord departed from His
disciples and ascended to the right hand of the Father to do the
work of intercession. He left His disciples on the earth to take
the journey He had assigned them.

[According to verse 47]…it was nightfall, and the boat was in the midst of the sea.…From the ascension of Christ to His coming again, this world is in a long night.…"The night is far advanced" (Rom. 13:12).…We are now in the night. This is why we see darkness all around us.

"The boat was in the midst of the sea." We still have not reached the destination of our journey.…The boat…has not arrived in port. There is still the danger and possibility of changing. We should not be overly self-assured and should not presume that our ending is already determined.

[The disciples] were "distressed as they rowed, for the wind was contrary to them."…If the journey which many Christians take is not contrary to the wind, I doubt whether such a journey is ordained by the Lord. We should take the journey that the Lord has ordained.…If we stand firmly on the course which the Lord has ordained, we will realize that the wind is contrary and indeed distressing!

The disciples were rowing from the evening to the fourth watch of the night.…The fourth watch is probably three o'clock in the morning,…the darkest hour of the night; it is the very end of the night.

The Lord…pays attention to every step we take. He knows how great our temptations are and how difficult our circumstances are. He will not let us endure beyond the fourth watch. When the night is far advanced, He comes to us. He has died for us and ascended to the heavens to pray for us. At the same time, He sees our hardship. When the night is far advanced, He will come.

[According to verse 51], as soon as the Lord comes, everything is fine. Thank and praise the Lord, the wind may be contrary, but it will not remain contrary forever. Though rowing is a toil, we will not need to row forever. (*The Collected Works of Watchman Nee,* vol. 10, pp. 424-427, 429-430)

Further Reading: The Collected Works of Watchman Nee, vol. 10, pp. 423-433

Enlightenment and inspiration: _____

_____

_____

_____

Morning Nourishment

Mark 1:15 And saying, The time is fulfilled and the kingdom of God has drawn near. Repent and believe in the gospel.

As used in Mark 1:15, the word "repent" literally means to think differently afterward, that is, to have a change of mind. To repent is to have a change of mind with regret for the past and a turn for the future. To repent before God is, on the negative side, to repent not only of sins and wrongdoings, but also to repent of the world and its corruption that usurp and corrupt people whom God made for Himself, and to repent of our God-forsaking life in the past. On the positive side, to repent is to turn to God in every way and in everything for fulfilling His purpose in making mankind. This is a "repentance unto God"; it is to "repent and turn to God" (Acts 20:21; 26:20). (*Life-study of Mark*, p. 49)

Today's Reading

[To repent] means to have a change of mind issuing in regret, to have a turn in purpose.…It is not to improve or reform oneself nor to forsake the evil and turn to the good, as people generally believe. Since the fall of man, man's mind has been turned against God and directed toward many persons, things, and matters other than God. Furthermore, man is controlled by his mind, doing the desires of the thoughts (Eph. 2:3). The desires of man's thoughts, whether they are good or bad, are always contrary to God and are directed toward persons, things, and matters other than God. Because of this, man also behaves himself in a way that is contrary to God and is thus directed toward persons, things, and matters other than God. Therefore, man should repent and have a change in his mind so that his conduct and behavior may also change accordingly.

Man's repentance is also his turning from things other than God to the kingdom of God.…God's New Testament economy is focused on His kingdom. For this we should repent, change our mind, have a turn in our pursuit and purpose of life, turning from persons, things, and matters other than God to the kingdom of God, that we may live under the ruling, the reigning, of God.

Man's repentance is also his turning from all things to God Himself (Acts 26:20; 14:15b; 1 Thes. 1:9b). Originally man's mind was toward all things outside of God; hence, under its direction, all of man's behavior and actions were also against God. Under the control of his mind, fallen man is against God in all things. Just as man's committing sins and doing evil are contrary to God, so also are his doing good and practicing justice. When man commits sin and does evil, he is turned toward evil and not toward God; in the same manner, when he does good and practices justice, he is turned toward goodness and justice and not toward God.

The repentance that God desires is that man would have a change of mind and turn toward God. Such a repentance is not only to correct man's wrongdoings; it is even more to correct man's condition of rejecting God and being turned away from God. It is not only to change evil into good; it is even more to turn the mind from things other than God to God. Therefore, even those who are considered to be right and good in the eyes of men also need to repent in this way. They need to have a change of mind, turning from the right and the good to God. A person's repentance is nothing less than his change from rejecting God and being turned against God to desiring God and being turned toward God. Real repentance should be a repentance unto God (Acts 20:21), a turning in reality from all things to God.

In God's New Testament economy, God charges all men everywhere to repent (Acts 17:30)....We must repent to God and turn to Him that we may believe in the gospel (Mark 1:15), believe in the Lord Jesus, receive Him as our Savior (Acts 20:21), enjoy God's salvation, and receive the gift of the Holy Spirit. Therefore, repentance is a divine requirement of God's New Testament economy.

Since repentance is a divine requirement of God's New Testament economy, it is a main item which we must proclaim concerning God's New Testament economy. (*Truth Lessons, Level One,* vol. 3, pp. 49-51, 53-54)

Further Reading: Truth Lessons, Level One, vol. 3, lsn. 29

Enlightenment and inspiration: _____

_____

_____

_____

Morning Nourishment

Mark ...Simon's mother-in-law was lying down with a fever,
1:30-31 ...and He came to *her* and raised her up, holding her
hand, and the fever left her...
42 And...the leprosy left him, and he was cleansed.
2:10-11 ...He said to the paralytic, to you I say, Rise, take up
your mat and go to your house.
5:29 ...Immediately the fountain of her blood was dried up...

Mark gives us a full portrait of how Jesus as the slave of God serves a sinner. I do not say sinners because all the pieces in this book should be considered as a collective case. Do not consider Peter's mother-in-law as an individual person sick of fever. She is a part of the sick person. Do not consider the leper as a separate individual. He also is a part of one complete sick person. In other words, the book of Mark shows us a complete sick person who was sick of fever (1:29-31), sick of leprosy (1:40-45), sick of paralysis (2:1-12), and sick of a flow of blood (5:25-34). This is a four-fold sickness. In the entire book of Mark you cannot find a fifth sickness. You may ask concerning the one with the withered hand (3:1). That case does not show the person who was sick; it only shows one of his members being sick. For example, with the blind the eyes are sick, with the deaf the ears are sick, and with the dumb the mouth is sick. However, the entire being, the entire person, is sick of only four kinds of diseases according to Mark—fever, leprosy, paralysis, and the flow of blood, the issue of blood. (*Elders' Training, Book 3: The Way to Carry Out the Vision*, p. 20)

Today's Reading

After the healing of the entire person, there is the exposure of the real inner being, the heart, in [Mark 7] (vv. 1-23). The heart is seen in chapter seven as something that is dirty and contaminated with nothing good and nothing pure. This is the inside, real situation and condition of such a fallen and sick person. The one who is sick of fever, leprosy, paralysis, and the flow of blood is rotten, dirty, and contaminated within his heart. Then this dirty inside was cleansed. Following this is a case of feeding—the feeding of the children and the pet dogs (7:27). Accompanying this sort of feeding are two miracles of feeding—the feeding of five thousand (6:30-44) and the feeding of four thousand (8:1-9).

We should not consider Peter, James, and John as individuals in the bird's-eye view of Mark....They are part of the same person. This person was healed from his fever, cleansed from his leprosy, recovered from his paralysis, and rescued from his issue of blood. He was exposed in his inner being and he was fed....Only such a person who passed through this marvelous process is qualified to go up to the Mount of Transfiguration [9:2-13].

At this point this person is healed, made alive, and cleansed inside, but he is still deaf, dumb, and blind. At this point what this man needs is a listening ear to be able to listen to the heavenly speaking (7:31-37). This is so that he will not speak nonsensically any longer. He speaks nonsensically because he never hears (7:32). He needs the healing of his ears to hear clearly. Then he needs the healing of his mouth to be able to speak properly and the healing of his eyes so that he can see [8:22-26]. It was on the Mount of Transfiguration that the need of the healing of the listening organ, speaking organ, and seeing organ began. When you were healed from the general diseases, were made alive, and were fed, you were able to go with the Lord to the mountain of transfiguration. Now you need to see and you need to hear the heavenly voice. You need to see that Christ is unique and that He is the unique replacement to replace everything, including you. Do not propose the building of three tabernacles the way Peter did on the mount. There is not one tabernacle for the law, one for the prophets, one for Christendom, or one for human culture. We must hear Him and we need such a hearing ear to hear Him. Do not hear culture; do not hear the prophets; do not hear the law; do not hear Moses or Elijah; do not hear anyone. "Hear Him!" (*Elders' Training, Book 3: The Way to Carry Out the Vision*, pp. 20-22)

Further Reading: Elders' Training, Book 3: The Way to Carry Out the Vision, chs. 1-2

Enlightenment and inspiration: _____

_____
_____
_____

Morning Nourishment

Mark For He was teaching His disciples. And He said to
9:31 them, The Son of Man is being delivered into the
hands of men, and they will kill Him; and when He
has been killed, after three days He will rise.
16:19-20 So then the Lord Jesus, after speaking to them, was
taken up into heaven and sat at the right hand of
God. And they went out and preached everywhere,
the Lord working with *them* and confirming the
word by the accompanying signs.

From Mark 9 onward Jesus brought His disciples with Him to bring them into Himself, to bring them into His death, and to bring them into His resurrection. To get into Christ you must go through His death and resurrection. Then you will reach Him. By this we can see how wonderful this book is.

In the last four or five chapters...[of Mark, the disciples were with the Lord] wherever He went and whatever He did....Do you realize that when Jesus died on the cross Peter was there? Jesus went to the cross with Peter. Probably Peter did not realize this, but he was brought there (Gal. 2:20). Jesus brought Peter and the other disciples into His death, into the tomb, into His resurrection, and into His ascension. Therefore, Peter and the others eventually became absolutely in Jesus Christ. Then they could carry out Jesus' commission. Now all of them are able to do what Jesus did in chapter one. In chapter one there is only one Jesus, but in chapter sixteen there are many reproductions of Jesus. (*Elders' Training, Book 3: The Way to Carry Out the Vision,* p. 22)

Today's Reading

Here is a full portrait of a person sick of fever, leprosy, paralysis, and an issue of blood. Such a person was dying but he was made alive, he was healed of all his diseases, he was cleansed within, he was fed, and he went up to the mountain with Jesus. However, he still needed to hear, to speak, and to see, so Jesus healed all the organs related to these functions (Mark 7:31-37; 8:22-26; 9:14-29; 10:46-52). Now this person began to hear the voice from the heavens, to speak the proper thing, and to see the vision. Jesus brought this person into His death (15:16-41) and into His resurrection (16:1-18), and this person ascended to the heavens in Jesus Christ (16:19). Then this collective person came down to preach the gospel just as Jesus did (16:20). This is a bird's-eye view of the entire book of Mark. This is not merely a history or a story but the divine significance of Mark.

We cannot be represented by one case. The Lord Jesus needed four gospels, and we need four "gospels" too. Our "gospels" are negative gospels. He has four sides and we have four sides too: one side is abnormality, another side is that we are dirty and contaminated, a third side is that we are paralyzed, not able to walk or do anything, and the fourth side is that we are leaking life. We are not living, but we are dying. The case of the woman with the flow of blood is merged with the case of a girl who died at twelve years of age (5:21-43). Her death is at the end of the twelfth year of the woman's flow of blood. This indicates that the flow of blood issues in death. We were abnormal persons, dirty, unclean, paralyzed and dying. However, the Slave-Savior, the Slave of God...healed us and... saved us from our sick condition. We were healed from all our diseases, cleansed from within and fed by the Lord. We became a pleasant person like Peter, James, and John. We all were qualified to go up the mountain but we got there blind, deaf, and unable to speak. We were healed and made alive, but we still did not have the seeing, speaking, and hearing ability. We needed the further healing of our organs. At this juncture Jesus was transfigured before them and Christ was unveiled because by this time they were healed in their hearing and seeing organs. They could hear and they could see so the Lord brought this collective person all the way to the cross and entered into resurrection and ascension. ...We need such a bird's-eye view of every book of the Bible. (*Elders' Training, Book 3: The Way to Carry Out the Vision*, pp. 22-24)

Further Reading: *Elders' Training, Book 3: The Way to Carry Out the Vision*, ch. 2; *Life-study of Mark*, msgs. 60, 63

Enlightenment and inspiration: _____

_____

_____

_____

What Miracle! What Mystery!

1   What miracle! What mystery!
     That God and man should blended be!
     God became man to make man God,
     Untraceable economy!
     From His good pleasure, heart's desire,
     His highest goal attained will be.

2   Flesh He became, the first God-man,
     His pleasure that I God may be:
     In life and nature I'm God's kind,
     Though Godhead's His exclusively.
     His attributes my virtues are;
     His glorious image shines through me.

3   No longer I alone that live,
     But God together lives with me.
     Built with the saints in the Triune God,
     His universal house we'll be,
     And His organic Body we
     For His expression corp'rately.

4   Jerusalem, the ultimate,
     Of visions the totality;
     The Triune God, tripartite man—
     A loving pair eternally—
     As man yet God they coinhere,
     A mutual dwelling place to be;
     God's glory in humanity
     Shines forth in splendor radiantly!

*Composition for prophecy with main point and
sub-points:* _____

_____
_____
_____
_____
_____
_____
_____
_____
_____
_____
_____
_____
_____
_____
_____
_____
_____
_____
_____
_____
_____
_____
_____
_____
_____
_____
_____
_____
_____
_____
_____
_____
_____
_____
_____
_____
_____
_____
_____

The Slave of God

Scripture Reading: Mark 10:45; Phil. 2:5-9; Isa. 42:1-4;
50:4-5, 7; Exo. 21:1-6

Day 1

I. **The subject of the Gospel of Mark is the Slave of God as the Slave-Savior of sinners (10:45):**

A. Mark's purpose is to provide a detailed record to show the beauty of the Lord Jesus as the Slave of God in His human virtues (5:34; 6:34; 8:23; 10:14-16).

B. In New Testament usage, the word *slave* refers to one who has sold himself and has lost all human rights (Rom. 1:1; 2 Pet. 1:1; Jude 1; Rev. 1:1):

1. When the Lord Jesus was on earth, He was a slave who had no rights.

2. In His gospel service He was a slave not only to God but also to man (Matt. 20:28; Phil. 2:7; Acts 3:13).

C. A key to understanding the Gospel of Mark is that in this Gospel we see much more of the Lord's acts than of His words (3:10-11; 4:39; cf. Acts 10:36-42).

D. Mark's record concerning Christ as the Slave of God is a record of the Lord's excellent deeds, which displayed both His lovely humanity in its virtue and perfection and His deity in its glory and honor (1:14-15, 21-22, 25-26, 30-31, 38-41; 2:10-11; 7:31-37).

E. Mark 10:45 reveals that, as the Slave of God, He served sinners even with His life, His soul; by giving His life as a ransom for sinners, the Lord Jesus accomplished the eternal purpose of God, whom He served as a slave.

F. As the Slave of God, the Lord Jesus taught His disciples, at the very time they were striving to be first, to take the position of a slave (vv. 35-45).

Day 2   **II. In the Gospel of Mark are the details of the teaching regarding Christ as the Slave of God in Philippians 2:5-9:**

A. Although the Lord was equal with God, He did not consider being equal with God a treasure to be grasped and retained; rather, He laid aside the form of God and emptied Himself, taking the form of a slave (vv. 6-7).

B. In His incarnation the Lord Jesus did not alter His divine nature; He changed only His outward expression, from the form of God, the highest form, to that of a slave, the lowest form (v. 7).

C. Christ's work in His human living to build up the fashion of a man and take on the form of a slave was the foundation and background of His ministry (v. 8a).

D. The Lord Jesus humbled Himself, "becoming obedient even unto death, and that the death of a cross," which was the climax of His humiliation (v. 8b).

E. The Lord humbled Himself to the uttermost, but God exalted Him to the highest peak (v. 9).

Day 3   F. The pattern presented in Philippians 2:5-9 is now the life within us; there is an urgent need among us to experience Christ as such a pattern.

G. "Let this mind be in you, which was also in Christ Jesus" (v. 5):

1. This is the mind that was in Christ when He emptied Himself, taking the form of a slave, and humbled Himself, being found in fashion as a man (vv. 5-8).

2. To have such a mind requires us to be one with Christ in His inward parts, in His tender inward feeling and in His thinking (1:8).

Day 4   **III. In the Gospel of Mark is the fulfillment of the detailed prophecies in Isaiah concerning Christ as the Slave of Jehovah; by considering these prophecies, we can understand** more fully what is recorded in Mark concerning Christ as a slave:

A. Jesus Christ, the Slave of God, was God's choice; God delighted in Him (Isa. 42:1).

B. The Lord's life was a life of sorrows and grief (53:2-3).

C. Instead of crying out and making His voice heard in the street, He was calm and quiet; He did not strive with others or promote Himself (42:2; Matt. 12:18-21).

D. Because He was full of mercy, He would not break those who are like a bruised reed, which cannot give a musical sound, or quench the ones who are like burning flax, which cannot give forth a shining light (Isa. 42:3-4).

E. The Lord Jesus did not speak His own word, but having the tongue of the instructed, He spoke according to God's instructions (50:4-5):

   1. The Lord Jehovah awakened Him every morning, awakening His ear to hear as an instructed one (v. 4b).

   2. The Lord Jesus was never rebellious; rather, He was always obedient, listening to the word of God (v. 5).

   3. Because the Lord Jesus had the ear and the tongue of an instructed one, He knew how "to sustain the weary with a word" (v. 4a).

F. The Slave-Savior trusted in God and set His face like a flint; in fulfilling God's purpose, He was strong (v. 7).

Day 5   IV. **The servant in Exodus 21:1-6 is a type of Christ as the Slave of God, who sacrificed Himself to serve God and God's people (Matt. 20:28; Eph. 5:2, 25):**

A. As the Slave of God, the Lord Jesus stood in the position of doing nothing on His own but acting only according to the word of the Father (Exo. 21:6; Psa. 40:6; John 5:19, 30, 36; 6:38; 7:16; 8:26; 12:49; 17:4).

B. Love is the motive and the prerequisite for a slave's continual service (Exo. 21:5); because the Lord Jesus loved the Father (His Master—John 14:31), the church (His wife—Eph. 5:25), and all the believers (His children—Gal. 2:20b; Eph. 5:2), He was willing to serve as a slave.

Day 6

C. All who believe in Christ, belong to Him, and have His serving life should take Him as their pattern by learning to be slaves, loving God, the church, and God's people (Mark 10:42-45; Phil. 2:5-8; Gal. 5:13; Eph. 5:2; Rom. 1:1):

    1. A slave does not care for his own interests but is always willing to empty himself, humble himself, lower himself, sacrifice himself, and serve others.

    2. As a slave of Christ and of God, Paul was willing to empty himself, humble himself, and sacrifice his rank, rights, and privileges (1 Cor. 9:19-23).

    3. Like Paul, we can become such slaves by the serving and sacrificing life of Christ (2 Cor. 12:15; Phil. 2:17).

    4. In carrying out God's New Testament economy, we need to have the spirit of a slave, the love of a slave, and the obedience of a slave (v. 5; Rev. 22:3b).

Morning Nourishment

Mark   And whoever wants to be first among you shall be
10:44-45   the slave of all. For even the Son of Man did not
come to be served, but to serve and to give His life
as a ransom for many.
Rom.   Paul, a slave of Christ Jesus, a called apostle, sepa-
1:1   rated unto the gospel of God.

The record concerning Christ as the Slave of God in the Gospel of Mark is not mainly a record of His wonderful words. Instead, it is a record of the Lord's excellent deeds. These deeds displayed both His lovely humanity in its virtue and perfection and His deity in its glory and honor.

The Gospel of Mark presents the Lord Jesus as a Slave of God and as the Slave-Savior of sinners. As the Slave-Savior, the Lord served sinners and gave His life as a ransom for them (10:45). By giving His life as a ransom for sinners, the Lord as the Slave-Savior accomplished the eternal purpose of God, whom He served as a Slave. (*Life-study of Mark*, p. 18)

Today's Reading

In His human living Christ took the form of a slave, serving God and men (Phil. 2:7; Acts 3:13; Mark 10:45). He was a slave not only to God but also to man. In New Testament usage, the word "slave" refers to one who has sold himself and has lost all human rights. When the Lord Jesus was on earth as a man, He was such a person. He was a slave who had no rights.

Speaking of Christ, Philippians 2:7 says that He "emptied Himself, taking the form of a slave, becoming in the likeness of men." The Greek word rendered "form" in this verse is the same word used for the form of God in Philippians 2:6. In His incarnation the Lord did not alter His divine nature but only His outward expression of the form of God to that of a slave. This was not a change of essence but of appearance.

The Gospel of Mark presents the Lord Jesus as the Slave of God. Because Mark presents Christ as a slave, he does not tell us His genealogy and status, for the ancestry of a slave is not worthy of note. Neither does Mark intend to impress us with the Slave's wonderful words (as Matthew does with His marvelous teachings and parables concerning the heavenly kingdom, and John with his profound revelations of divine truths), but with His deeds in His gospel service. Concerning this, the Gospel of Mark provides more details than the other Gospels in order to portray Christ's diligence, faithfulness, and other virtues in the saving service He rendered to sinners for God. In Mark's Gospel is the fulfillment of the prophecy concerning Christ as the Slave of Jehovah in Isaiah 42:1-4, 6-7; 49:5-7; 50:4-7; 52:13—53:12 and the details of the teaching regarding Christ as the Slave of God in Philippians 2:5-11. Such a Slave served sinners as their Savior with His life as their ransom (Mark 10:45), for the fulfillment of the eternal purpose of God, whose Slave He was.

In Mark 10:45 the Lord Jesus says, "The Son of Man did not come to be served, but to serve and to give His life as a ransom for many." This is a very strong expression stating that Christ, as the Son of Man in His humanity, is the Slave of God to serve sinners even with His life, His soul. Furthermore, the word "ransom" here indicates that even the Lord's redemption was His service rendered to sinners for God's plan.

The believers are also slaves of God. Romans 6:22 says that we have been "enslaved to God." First Peter 2:16 says, "As free, and yet not having freedom as a covering for evil, but as slaves of God." One aspect of our status as believers is that we are priests of God; another aspect is that we are slaves of God. We should be happy to be both priests and slaves. Actually, the Greek word rendered "slaves" in 1 Peter 2:16 means bondslaves. A bondslave, according to ancient custom and law, was one who was purchased by his master and over whom his master had absolute rights, even to the extent of terminating his life. As believers we are such bondslaves of God. (*The Conclusion of the New Testament,* pp. 296-297, 1099)

Further Reading: Life-study of Mark, msg. 1; *The Conclusion of the New Testament,* msgs. 70, 102

Enlightenment and inspiration: _____

_____

_____

_____

Morning Nourishment

**Phil. But emptied Himself, taking the form of a slave,
2:7-9 becoming in the likeness of men; and being found
in fashion as a man, He humbled Himself, becoming
obedient even unto death, and *that* the death of a cross.
Therefore also God highly exalted Him and bestowed
on Him the name which is above every name.**

[In Philippians 2:5-11 there are two sections.] The first section
is on Christ emptying Himself [vv. 5-7]. The second section is on
Christ humbling Himself [vv. 8-11]. The Lord lowered Himself
twice, first in emptying Himself in His deity, and then in humbling Himself in His humanity. When the Lord came down to
earth, He emptied Himself of the glory, power, position, and image
in His deity. As a result of His emptying, those without revelation did not recognize Him and would not acknowledge Him as
God, considering Him merely to be an ordinary man. In the Godhead the Lord voluntarily chose to be the Son, submitting
Himself to the authority of the Father. Hence, He said that the
Father was greater than He (John 14:28). The Son's position was
a voluntary choice of our Lord. In the Godhead there is full
harmony. In the Godhead there is equality, yet it is happily
arranged that the Father should be the Head and that the Son
should submit. The Father became the representation of authority, and the Son became the representation of submission.
(Watchman Nee, *Authority and Submission,* pp. 41-42)

Today's Reading

In His human living Christ was found in fashion as a man,
even in the form of a slave....The likeness of men denotes the outward appearance of His humanity. He appeared outwardly to men
as a man, but inwardly He had the reality of deity. Furthermore,
when Christ became in the likeness of men, entering into the condition of humanity, He was found in fashion as a man by men.

Philippians 2:7 says that Christ even took the form of a slave.
In His incarnation the Lord Jesus did not alter His divine nature
but only His outward expression of the form of God (Phil. 2:6) to

that of a slave. This was not a change of essence but of state. Before His incarnation [Christ] was, of course, not in fashion as a man. He was only in the form of God. But after He became a man it was necessary for Him to live and work in such a way as to build up the fashion of man in order to be found by others in fashion as a man. It took the Lord Jesus thirty years to build up such a fashion of man in His human living. Therefore, this should be considered part of His work in His human living.

While the Lord Jesus was living in His humanity on earth, He was working to build up the fashion of man. The Lord did not simply behave like a man for a short period of time. He became a man and then lived a human life for thirty years, living in the poor and lowly home of a carpenter. As He lived there, He built up the fashion of man and was found in fashion as a man. The Lord, therefore, carried out the great work of building up a human fashion...during the first thirty years of His human life.

Christ did not work to build up the fashion of a highly exalted man or of a man with a high rank. On the contrary, He worked to build up the fashion of a man who was a slave. It was not an easy thing that the Lord Jesus built up a fashion of a man in such a low state. This was a very fine work, and it took Him thirty years to accomplish it in full. After He finished this work, He came forth to begin His ministry. His ministry was based upon His work of building up in Himself the fashion of a man.

It is crucial for us to see that Christ's work in His human living to build up the fashion of a man and to take on the form of a slave was the foundation and background of His ministry. Those who aspire to serve the Lord need to have a work not by doing but by living. This is a work carried out by one's daily living. Those who wish to serve the Lord need to live to build up a work that will be the solid ground and strong background for their coming service to the Lord. (*The Conclusion of the New Testament*, pp. 684-685)

Further Reading: Authority and Submission, ch. 5; The Conclusion of the New Testament, msg. 64

Enlightenment and inspiration: _____

_____

_____

_____

Morning Nourishment

Phil. **For God is my witness how I long after you all in the**
1:8 **inward parts of Christ Jesus.**
2:5-6 **Let this mind be in you, which was also in Christ**
Jesus, who, existing in the form of God, did not con-
sider being equal with God a treasure to be grasped.

Let us now consider Philippians 2:5 through 8 in more
detail. In verse 5 Paul says, "Let this mind be in you, which was
also in Christ Jesus." The Greek words translated "let this
mind be in you" can also be rendered "think this in you." The
word "this" refers to the counting and regarding in verses 3
and 4. This kind of thinking, mind, attitude, was also in Christ
when He emptied Himself, taking the form of a slave, and humbled Himself, being found in fashion as a man (vv. 7-8). To have
such a mind requires us to be one with Christ in His inward
parts (1:8). To experience Christ, we need to be one with Him to
such an extent, that is, in His tender inward feeling and in His
thinking. (*Life-study of Philippians*, p. 86)

Today's Reading

The Lord's humiliation involves seven steps: emptying
Himself, taking the form of a slave, becoming in the likeness of
men, humbling Himself, becoming obedient, being obedient
even unto death, and being obedient unto the death of the
cross.

The pattern presented in these verses is now the life within
us. This life is what we call a crucified life. The seven steps
of Christ's humiliation are all aspects of the crucified life.
Although Christ had the expression of deity, He laid aside this
expression. However, He did not lay aside the reality of His
deity. He laid aside the higher form, the form of God, and took
on a much lower form, the form of a slave. In this, He emptied
Himself. Surely this is a mark of a crucified life. Then, after
becoming a man and being found in the appearance of a man,
Christ humbled Himself even unto the death of the cross. This
was the crucified life lived out in a full and absolute way.

Christ is not only an outward pattern for us; He is also the life within us. As this inner life, He would have us experience Him and thereby live a crucified life. In this crucified life there is no room for rivalry, vainglory, or self-exaltation. On the contrary, there is self-emptying and self-humbling. Whenever we experience Christ and live Christ, we automatically live such a crucified life. This means that when we live Christ, we live the One who is the pattern of a crucified life. Then we also shall empty ourselves and humble ourselves.

We should take the crucified life in 2:5-8 as our pattern so that we can experience the power of resurrection which exalted Christ to the highest peak in the universe. The experience of Christ as the pattern of a crucified life and the experience of the resurrection power which exalts Him is endless. Day by day, we need to live a crucified life. This is to live Christ as our pattern. Instead of having a life of rivalry and vainglory, we should live a life of self-emptying and self-humbling. This is to live a crucified life. By means of this life we are ushered into the power of resurrection by which Christ is exalted.

There is an urgent need among us in the Lord's recovery today to experience Christ as our pattern. We desperately need to experience Him as our crucified life. Such a life stands altogether in contrast to a life of rivalry and vainglory. In the church life we either take the crucified life as our pattern or automatically live a life of rivalry and vainglory. There is no third way. If we do not take the crucified life as our pattern, we shall automatically live in the way of rivalry for vainglory. The issue here is extremely serious. We need to be honest with ourselves and consider the kind of life we have been living in the church. If you review the time you have been in the church life, you will see that whenever you did not take the crucified life as your pattern, you were living a life of rivalry for vainglory. (*Life-study of Philippians,* pp. 88-89, 91-92)

Further Reading: Life-study of Philippians, msgs. 10-11

Enlightenment and inspiration: _____

_____

_____

_____

Morning Nourishment

Isa. **He will not cry out, nor lift up *His voice*,**
42:2 **Nor make His voice heard in the street.**
   3 **A bruised reed He will not break;**
      And a dimly burning flax He will not extinguish;
      He will bring forth justice in truth.
   4 **He will not faint, nor will He be discouraged...**
50:4 **The Lord Jehovah has given me**
      The tongue of the instructed,
      That I should know how to sustain the weary with
      a word.
      He awakens *me* morning by morning;
      He awakens my ear
      To hear as an instructed one.

Isaiah 42:1 says, "Here is My Servant, whom I uphold, / My
chosen One in whom My soul delights." Jesus Christ, the Slave
of God, was God's choice from among billions of human beings.
Because He was God's choice, God delighted in Him. Hence, He
became the delight of God's heart.

Verse 2 indicates that the Lord did not cry or lift up His voice.
...This means that the Lord did not shout or make noise. Instead
of crying out to make His voice known in the streets, He was
calm and quiet. (*Life-study of Mark,* pp. 9, 11)

Today's Reading

According to Isaiah 42:3,...the Lord would not break a
bruised reed or quench a dimly burning flax. The Jews often
made flutes of reeds. When a reed was bruised and no longer
useful as a musical instrument, they broke it. They also made
torches with flax to burn with oil. When the oil ran out, the flax
smoked, and they quenched it. Some of the Lord's people are like
a bruised reed that cannot give a musical sound; others are like
smoking flax that cannot give a shining light. Yet the Lord
would not "break" the bruised ones who cannot give a musical
sound or quench the ones like dimly burning flax that cannot
give a shining light. On the one hand, the Lord would not break
a bruised reed or quench a dimly burning flax. On the other

hand, according to verse 4, He would not faint as a dimly burning flax, nor would He be crushed as a bruised reed.

From Isaiah 50:4 we see that as the Slave of God the Lord was given the tongue of the instructed....Although as a Slave, the Lord was not a teaching one, He was nonetheless given the tongue of the instructed. He was instructed by God to know how to sustain a weary one with a word. Because He had been instructed by God, He could sustain a weary one by giving him a single word. Such a word is able to minister life more than a long message.

Isaiah 50:7 says, "The Lord Jehovah helps me; / Therefore I have not been dishonored; / Therefore I have set my face like a flint, / And I know that I will not be put to shame." Here we see that the Lord trusted in God and set His face like a flint. As the Lord Jesus was walking in God's way to fulfill God's will, His face was like a hard stone. In the matter of fulfilling God's will He was very strong. (*Life-study of Mark,* pp. 11-13)

Christ as the Servant of Jehovah was instructed not by man but by God. Christ did not speak His own word but spoke according to God's instructions. He thus learned how to sustain the weary ones, the weak ones, with a word. Jehovah awakened Him every morning. This indicates that every day the Lord Jesus had a morning revival. Furthermore, the Lord was never rebellious; rather, He was always obedient, listening to the word of God.

As the instructed ones, we need to be awakened by the Lord morning by morning. This is the real morning revival. He awakens our ear to hear as an instructed one. When the Lord Jehovah opens our ear and speaks to us, we should not be rebellious or turn back. We should take His word and obey. This was Isaiah's attitude as a learner serving Jehovah. This also typifies Christ. The four Gospels show that the Lord Jesus held such an attitude. (*Life-study of Isaiah,* pp. 173-174, 326)

Further Reading: Life-study of Isaiah, msgs. 22, 25, 45

Enlightenment and inspiration: _____

_____

_____

_____

Morning Nourishment

Exo.   But if the servant plainly says, I love my master, my wife,
21:5-6   and my children; I will not go out free; then his master
shall bring him to God and shall bring him to the door
or to the doorpost, and his master shall bore his ear
through with an awl; and he shall serve him forever.
Eph.   And walk in love, even as Christ also loved us and
5:2   gave Himself up for us, an offering and a sacrifice to
God for a sweet-smelling savor.

The Bible reveals that as believers in Christ, we are not only
God's creatures, but also God's sons. In the old creation we are
creatures of God; in the new creation we have become sons of God.
However, if we maintain our rank as creatures and sons, we shall
not be able to keep God's word. To keep His word, we need to
empty ourselves and humble ourselves, laying aside the rank
both of a creature and of a son. Then we shall be slaves with God
as our Master. According to the type in Exodus 21, Christ is the
slave, and God is the Master. If we would take Christ as our
pattern, we must learn to be slaves, those who sacrifice everything for others. (*Life-study of Exodus*, p. 808)

Today's Reading

As One who Himself became a slave, the Lord Jesus taught
His disciples, at the very time they were striving to be first, to take
the position of a slave. He said to them, "Whoever wants to be first
among you shall be your slave; just as the Son of Man did not
come to be served, but to serve and to give His life as a ransom for
many" (Matt. 20:27-28).

According to Exodus 21:2, a Hebrew slave was to be set free
after serving his master six years. If he obtained a wife and children during his years as a slave, he was to leave them as the prop-
erty of his master and "go out by himself" (v. 4). However, the slave
might plainly say, "I love my master, my wife, and my children; I
will not go out free" (v. 5). Here we see that continuing as a slave is
not a legal requirement; it is a matter of love. Because the slave
loved his master, his wife, and his children, he did not want to go

out free. Instead, he would serve his master forever. Love is the basis of his continued service.

It is often said that love blinds people. In a very real sense, if we would love others, we should be blind toward them. Concerning ourselves, however, we must be a sacrifice. Love requires sacrifice. Without sacrifice, there can be no love. The Lord Jesus loved us by being a sacrifice for us [Eph. 5:2]....Christ gave Himself for us, dying a malefactor's death on the cross. This proves that love demands sacrifice.

If a brother is not willing to sacrifice himself, he cannot love his wife. Likewise, parents must be willing to sacrifice for their children if they are to love their children. There is no love without sacrifice.

According to Exodus 21:5, it was possible that a slave might not want to be free. Out of love for his master, wife, and children, he might prefer to remain under bondage as a slave. This is not a matter of legal requirement; it is motivated by voluntary love.

The Lord Jesus loves God, the church, and all His people. God is His Master, the church is His wife, and all His people are His children....According to John 14:31, the Lord loves the Father; according to Ephesians 5:25, Christ loves the church; and according to Galatians 2:20 and Ephesians 5:2, Christ loves all the believers, all the saints. Motivated by such a love, He was willing to be a slave. Love is the motive and the prerequisite of being a slave.

Exodus 21:6 speaks of the slave being brought to the door or to the doorpost. In ancient times slaves were to stand by the doorpost waiting for the master's orders. Instead of doing anything on their own, they were to act only according to the word of the master. Today our position as slaves of Christ should also be at the doorpost. Furthermore, in 21:6 we are told that the master bored his slave's ear through with an awl. This indicates that the slave's ear was opened to listen to the master. (*Life-study of Exodus,* pp. 809-810)

Further Reading: Life-study of Exodus, msg. 68; *Authority and Submission,* chs. 4, 7

Enlightenment and inspiration: _____

_____

_____

_____

Morning Nourishment

Mark **And Jesus called them to *Him* and said to them, You**
10:42-43 **know that those who are esteemed as rulers of the**
         Gentiles lord it over them, and their great ones exer-
         cise authority over them. But it is not so among you;
         but whoever wants to become great among you shall
         be your servant.

2 Cor. **But I, I will most gladly spend and be utterly spent**
12:15 **on behalf of your souls....**

Many Christians are serving God, but they do not stand by the doorpost, and their ear has not been bored through with an awl. They act on their own, not in accord with what they hear from the Master. They do many things according to their own concepts, desires, and intentions.

As those who believe in Christ, we all must be His slaves. We should say, "O Lord, I love You. Even if I have the freedom to go out, I do not want to leave. I love You, I love Your church, and I love Your children." On the one hand, we may testify of how enjoyable and glorious the church life is. On the other hand, in the church life we all must become slaves. The New Testament as well as the Old indicates that God's people need the spirit of a slave. (*Life-study of Exodus*, pp. 810-811)

Today's Reading

The elders in the churches need to realize that if they are not willing to be slaves, they cannot be proper elders. Every elder must be a slave. This was the reason the Lord Jesus taught His disciples not to seek to be above others, but instead to place themselves lower than others and be their slaves. In the church life there is no rank. We are all brothers, and we all must serve as slaves.

We have given hundreds of messages on life, the Spirit, Christ, and the church. However, if we would apply these messages, we must be slaves. Those who are not willing to have the spirit of a slave cannot enter into all these messages in a practical way. In the past certain ones testified that they loved the church and were willing to consecrate themselves to the church. However, eventually these very ones left the church life, and some even became opposers of the church. Deep within them they had the ambition for position. Because this ambition could not be fulfilled in the church life, they left the church. Only those who are willing to be slaves can remain permanently in the church life. No matter how I may be treated by the saints, I have no choice but to remain in the church life. The church is the home of my Father and of all His children. I am simply one of His slaves, loving Him, loving the church, and loving His children. After giving so many messages on life, the Spirit, Christ, and the church, I am glad to give this message on slavery. This word is for us all.

If we have the spirit of a slave and the love of a slave, it will be easy for us to obey. Love is always followed by obedience....In a very real sense, good parents must sometimes obey their children. Often parents obey their children more quickly than the children obey the parents. The point here is that love produces obedience. Only a slave can obey. A good parent is one who has the love and obedience of a slave. Deep within, a mother who loves her children is willing to be a slave to them and do anything for them....Love is the prerequisite of obedience.

My burden in this message has been to emphasize three matters: the spirit of a slave, the love of a slave, and the obedience of a slave. If we have [these], we shall be able to keep the commandments. At first, this word may sound strange. But if you consider it honestly, you will see that it is true in our practical experience. Only a person with the spirit, love, and obedience of a slave can keep God's ordinances. In the New Testament economy, as well as in the Old Testament, there is the need of such a spirit, love, and obedience.

As those who believe in Christ, belong to Him, and have His life of sacrifice, we also must be slaves loving God, the church, and God's people. With such a love as our motivation, we need to be slaves sacrificing and serving. (*Life-study of Exodus*, pp. 811-812)

Further Reading: Life-study of Mark, msg. 2; The Conclusion of the New Testament, msgs. 27, 69

Enlightenment and inspiration: _____

_____

_____

_____

Hymns, #463

1   I love, I love my Master,
     I will not go out free,
   For He is my Redeemer;
     He paid the price for me.
   I would not leave His service,
     It is so sweet and blest;
   And in the weariest moments
     He gives the truest rest.

2   My Master shed His life-blood
     My vassal life to win,
   And save me from the bondage
     Of tyrant self and sin.
   He chose me for His service,
     And gave me power to choose
   That blessed, perfect freedom,
     Which I shall never lose.

3   I would not halve my service,
     His only it must be!
   His only, who so loved me,
     And gave Himself for me.
   Rejoicing and adoring,
     Henceforth my song shall be,
   I love, I love my Master,
     I will not go out free.

Composition for prophecy with main point and sub-points: _____

_____

_____

_____

_____

_____

_____

_____

_____

_____

_____

_____

_____

_____

_____

_____

_____

_____

_____

_____

_____

_____

_____

_____

_____

_____

_____

_____

_____

_____

_____

_____

The Contents
of the Slave-Savior's Gospel Service

Scripture Reading: Mark 1:14-45

Day 1 **I. Christ as the Slave-Savior did not come to be served, but to serve; He served us in the past, He still serves us in the present, and He is going to serve us in the future (Mark 10:45; Luke 22:26-27; 12:37):**

A. The story of the gospel and the meaning of salvation are that Christ loves and serves us first, and then we love and serve Him; whenever we have a need, we can come to the Lord and let Him serve us so that He can serve others through us (Matt. 26:13; 1 John 4:19; John 13:12-17; Rom. 1:1; Gal. 6:17; 1 John 3:16).

B. As the life-giving Spirit, the Slave-Savior serves us by dispensing Himself as life into us so that we can become the means by which He dispenses Himself as life into others (John 10:10b; 1 Cor. 15:45b; 1 John 5:16a; 2 Cor. 3:6).

Day 2 **II. We need to see and enter into the reality of the contents of the Slave-Savior's wonderful and excellent gospel service (Mark 1:14-45):**

A. The first thing the Slave-Savior did in His gospel service was to proclaim the gospel (vv. 14-20):

1. Christ Himself, with all the processes He passed through and all the redemptive work He accomplished, is the content of the gospel (v. 1).

2. Christ came not only as the Messenger of God, bringing a word or a message from God to God's people, but also as the message sent by God; He Himself is the living message of God (vv. 1-8; Mal. 3:1-3; cf. 4:1-2).

3. The Slave-Savior's proclaiming was to announce God's glad tidings to the miserable

people in bondage; His teaching (Mark 1:21-22) was to enlighten the ignorant ones in darkness with the divine light of the truth.

4. His proclaiming implied teaching, and His teaching implied proclaiming (Matt. 4:23; Mark 1:38-39; 3:14; 6:12; 14:9; 16:15, 20).

Day 3

B. The second thing the Slave-Savior did in His gospel service was to teach the truth (1:21-22):

1. The truth is the shining of the divine light on the facts of the Bible to televise a heavenly vision of those facts into our being; the truth is the shining of the light, the light is the light of life, and the life is the Spirit; thus, truth, life, and the Spirit (which are all Christ Himself) are inseparable (John 8:12, 32, 36; 1:4; 14:6a; 2 Cor. 3:6, 8, 17; cf. Rom. 8:2).

2. The Lord's teaching of the truth (Mark 2:13; 4:1; 6:2, 6, 30, 34; 10:1; 11:17; 12:35; 14:49) was to bring people out of the satanic darkness into the divine light (Acts 26:18); the Slave-Savior, as the light of the world (John 8:12; 9:5), came as a great light to Galilee, the land of darkness, to shine on the people who were sitting in the shadow of death (Matt. 4:12-16).

3. His teaching released the word of light to enlighten those in the darkness of death that they might receive the light of life (John 1:4).

Day 4

C. The third thing the Slave-Savior did in His gospel service was to cast out demons from the possessed people (Mark 1:23-28):

1. The demons' possession of people signifies Satan's usurpation of man, whom God created for His purpose.

2. The Lord Jesus came to destroy the works of Satan (1 John 3:8), and His casting out of demons (Mark 1:34, 39; 3:15; 6:7, 13; 16:17)

was for people to be delivered from Satan's
bondage (Luke 13:16), out of Satan's authority of darkness (Acts 26:18; Col. 1:13), into
God's kingdom (Mark 1:15).

D. The fourth thing the Slave-Savior did in His
gospel service was to heal the sick (vv. 29-39):

1. Sickness issues from sin and is a sign of
man's abnormal condition before God; the
Lord healed people's sick condition and
restored them to normality that they might
serve Him (v. 34; 3:10; 6:5, 13, 56).

2. We must learn to preach the gospel and
teach the truth like a physician, giving
people a heavenly prescription and the
divine medicine for their healing (Matt.
9:11-13; Luke 10:33-37; cf. Prov. 4:20-23;
Exo. 30:25).

Day 5   E. The fifth thing the Slave-Savior did in His
gospel service was to cleanse the leper (Mark
1:40-45):

1. Leprosy signifies the sin of rebellion, the
serious sin issuing from within man, such
as willful sin, presumptuous sin, and oppos-
ing God with determination (1 John 3:4;
cf. Isa. 14:12-15; Lev. 13:2; 14:9).

2. As seen in the cases of Miriam (Num. 12:1-
10), Gehazi (2 Kings 5:20-27), and Uzziah (2
Chron. 26:16-21), leprosy issues from rebellion against God's authority, God's deputy
authority, God's regulation, and God's economy.

3. In Leviticus 14:33-57 the house typifies
the church as our real home, and the
leprosy in the house signifies sins and
evils in the church; the priest signifies
the Lord or His deputy authority, and the
examining of the house is not for condemnation but is a grace for healing (1 Cor.
1:11):

Day 6

a. The removing of the infected stones after seven days (Lev. 14:40) signifies that after the observation of a complete period of time, if the problem of the church is still spreading, the believer or believers involved in the problem should be removed from the fellowship of the church and be considered unclean, like the outsiders; this is done to stop the spread of the disease and to eliminate the disease (Rom. 16:17; Titus 3:10).

b. Putting other stones in the place of the removed stones (Lev. 14:42a) signifies using other believers (1 Pet. 2:5) to fill in the gap; the replastering of the house with other plaster (Lev. 14:42b) signifies the renewing of the church with new experiences of the Lord's gracious works; this is needed for a new start in the church life.

c. The breaking down of the house after the infection of leprosy returns (v. 45) signifies that if the situation of a church reaches the point where it cannot be cured, that church should be terminated (cf. Rev. 2:5).

d. If no sin is spreading after the renewing of the church with the new experiences of the Lord's gracious works, the church is clean and has no problem; the whole church needs to be cleansed with the eternally efficacious blood of Christ and His eternal and living Spirit so that the church is fully clean to be the mutual dwelling of God and man (Lev. 14:48-53; Heb. 9:14; 10:22; 1 John 1:9; Titus 3:5; John 14:2, 23).

Morning Nourishment

Luke   But you shall not be so; but let the greatest among
22:26-27 you become like the youngest, and the one who
leads like the one who serves. For who is greater,
the one who reclines *at table* or the one who serves?
Is it not the one who reclines *at table?* But I am in
your midst as the one who serves.

12:37   Blessed are those slaves whom the master, when he
comes, will find watching. Truly I tell you that he
will gird himself and will have them recline *at table*,
and he will come to *them* and serve them.

Three passages...help us see how Christ served us in the past,
still serves us in the present, and is going to serve us in the future.

Let us consider the first passage: "For even the Son of Man did
not come to be served, but to serve and to give His life as a ransom
for many" (Mark 10:45). This verse mentions that the Son of Man
came to serve everybody. Whoever comes to the Lord, the Lord
always serves them. The Lord feeds the hungry; He heals the sick
ones. Without regard to the time and place, the Lord always serves
us. The highest service of the Lord was giving His life as a ransom
for many. He gave His life to serve man. So many times, we are so
eager to serve the Lord that we ignore the fact that our Lord went
to the cross and gave His life to serve us. While we were yet sinners,
He served us. (*The Collected Works of Watchman Nee*, vol. 17, p. 191)

Today's Reading

Let us consider the second passage:....(Luke 22:26-27) [above].
The book of Mark concerns Christ serving the sinners. Here it
concerns Christ serving His disciples. "I am in your midst as the
one who serves." We should remember that the Lord is among us
to serve us. This is grace!

The bread before us at the Lord's table clearly demonstrates
how Christ has served us. His body was broken for all of us. The
meaning of salvation is that Christ serves us first, and then we
serve Him. His serving does not end with the cross. Even now He
is among us to continue His service. Whenever we have a need,

we ought to come to the Lord and let Him serve us.

When you study the Gospels, do you sense that the Lord served His disciples step by step? You may be amazed and think that Christians ought to serve the Lord and wonder why the Lord would come to serve Christians! Why does the Lord want to serve the Christians? "For who is greater, the one who reclines at table or the one who serves? Is it not the one who reclines at table?" (Luke 22:27). This verse exposes the human concept. The Lord is in our midst as the One who serves. He is able to serve man because He is so great and is even the greatest. The greater we are, the more we can serve. The smaller we are, the less we can serve. Whoever is the smallest may not be able to serve a single person. The Lord is great; He is infinitely great and can therefore serve man in an infinite way.

We still have the third passage:....(Luke 12:37) [above]. This is too gracious! How can this be possible? However, the Lord said He will serve us again in the future. Once we were indebted to the Lord and received His grace freely. We will forever be indebted to the Lord and will forever enjoy His grace.

I wonder how many people know how to enjoy the service of Christ. Many times we are misled to think that we should serve Christ. Have we ever asked Christ to serve us? Some brothers have said that their prayers are too cold and that they have to do something to stir themselves up again. At such times they should realize that Christ can serve them in that very matter. Some have felt that they have no interest in the Bible and worry about what they should do the next day. They should realize that in that very matter, Christ can serve them also.

God has given Christ to us for the purpose of serving us. From the day that Christ was crucified on the cross until eternity, Christ will serve us. Although we do not quite understand this, we can enjoy it. (*The Collected Works of Watchman Nee*, vol. 17, pp. 191-194)

Further Reading: The Collected Works of Watchman Nee, vol. 17, pp. 191-194; *Basic Lessons on Service*, ch. 12

Enlightenment and inspiration: _____

_____

_____

_____

Morning Nourishment

Mark   **And after John was delivered up, Jesus came into**
1:14-15 **Galilee, proclaiming the gospel of God, and saying,**
The time is fulfilled and the kingdom of God has
drawn near. Repent and believe in the gospel.

38 **And He said to them, Let us go elsewhere into the**
nearby towns that I may preach there also, because
for this *purpose* **I came out.**

The beginning of the gospel is actually the ushering in of this
living Person. For us today, Christ is everything. As long as we
have Him, we have everything. We do not have promises—we
have Christ. We do not have prophecies—we have Christ. We do
not have types—we have Christ. We do not strive to keep the law,
because Christ is here, and we have Him. In our spiritual dictio-
nary the unique word is Christ. (*Life-study of Mark*, p. 42)

Today's Reading

Now that we have seen what the gospel is, we need to go on to
consider the contents of the gospel service revealed in 1:14-45.
According to this section of the Gospel of Mark, the contents of the
gospel service include five items: preaching the gospel (vv. 14-20),
teaching the truth (vv. 21-22), casting out demons (vv. 23-28),
healing the sick (vv. 29-39), and cleansing the leper (vv. 40-45).

According to Mark 1:14, Jesus came into Galilee preaching the
gospel of God. The Slave-Savior's preaching was to announce God's
glad tidings to the miserable people in bondage. His teaching
(vv. 21-22) was to enlighten the ignorant ones in darkness with
the divine light of the truth. His preaching implied teaching, and
His teaching implied preaching (Matt. 4:23). This is the first thing
He did in His ministry, and it was the all-embracing structure of
His evangelical service (Mark 1:38-39; 3:14; 6:12; 14:9; 16:15, 20).

The Lord's preaching always implied teaching, and His teaching implied preaching. This indicates something important
related to our gospel preaching today. Many saints are burdened
for the preaching of the gospel. They earnestly desire to preach
the gospel to their relatives, neighbors, friends, classmates, and

colleagues. However, many have had the experience of not knowing what to say when they try to preach the gospel. The reason for this is that they have not developed the skill to teach the gospel, although they have the burden to preach the gospel. If we do not know how to teach, we shall not be able to preach effectively. Gospel preaching depends on teaching.

Much of our gospel preaching has not been effective or fruitful. The reason for this lack of effectiveness or fruitfulness is that the preaching of some saints is lacking in content. When we speak to others, we need to have something rich to present to them.

As a Slave serving God, the Lord Jesus preached the gospel and taught the truth to the people who were ignorant and were in darkness. The church, as the continuation of the Lord, His enlargement and increase, should do the same thing today. To the fallen people in darkness, the church should preach the gospel and teach the truth. I hope that all the saints in the Lord's recovery will become good preachers of the gospel and good teachers of the Bible.

If we all become good preachers and teachers, the Lord will have a way to hasten His coming back....We need to be faithful to follow the Lord's steps in the matters of preaching the gospel and teaching the truth....I am especially hopeful that the young people will be faithful to the Lord in His recovery. Young people, there is a long way ahead of you. I urge you to be faithful in the Lord's recovery to preach the gospel and teach the truth.

Specifically, in Mark 1:15 the Lord Jesus preached that we should believe in the gospel. This is the gospel of Jesus Christ, the Son of God (v. 1), the gospel of God, and the gospel of the kingdom of God. Jesus Christ, the Son of God, with all the processes through which He has passed, including incarnation, crucifixion, resurrection, and ascension, and all the redemptive work He accomplished, is the contents of the gospel (Rom. 1:2-4; Luke 2:10-11; 1 Cor. 15:1-4; 2 Tim. 2:8). Hence the gospel is of Him. (*Life-study of Mark*, pp. 42-45, 47-48, 50)

Further Reading: Life-study of Mark, msgs. 4-5

Enlightenment and inspiration: _____

_____

_____

_____

Morning Nourishment

Mark 1:21-22   ...And immediately, on the Sabbath, He entered into the synagogue and taught. And they were astounded at His teaching, for He taught them as One having authority and not like the scribes.

John 8:32, 36   And you shall know the truth, and the truth shall set you free....If therefore the Son sets you free, you shall be free indeed.

In the synagogue, the Lord Jesus taught the people with authority. Man's fall into sin broke his fellowship with God. As a result, man became ignorant of the knowledge of God. Such ignorance issued first in darkness and then in death. The Slave-Savior, as the light of the world (John 8:12; 9:5), came to Galilee, the land of darkness, where people were sitting in the shadow of death, and He came as a great light to shine upon them (Matt. 4:12-16). His teaching released the word of light to enlighten those in the darkness of death so that they might receive the light of life (John 1:4). We have already seen that the first thing the Slave-Savior did in His service was to preach the gospel. Now the second thing the Slave of God as the Slave-Savior to fallen men did in His service was to carry out such teaching (Mark 2:13; 4:1; 6:2, 6, 30, 34; 10:1; 11:17; 12:35; 14:49) to bring people out of satanic darkness into the divine light (Acts 26:18). (*Life-study of Mark*, pp. 51-52)

Today's Reading

It was of God's sovereignty that the Lord Jesus was raised in the region of Galilee and also that He began His preaching and teaching not from Judea, but from Galilee....Galilee was not only a despised region, but was also a place of darkness....Matthew 4:15-16 says, "...Galilee of the Gentiles: The people sitting in darkness have seen a great light; and to those sitting in the region and shadow of death, to them light has risen." This indicates that when the Lord Jesus walked through Galilee, He was a great light shining in the darkness and shining upon the people sitting in the region and shadow of death. In particular, the teaching of the Slave-Savior was the shining of a great light. Every word that issued out of His mouth was an enlightening word. Therefore, while He was teaching the people, the light was shining upon them. In this way the people in darkness were enlightened by the Lord's teaching.

Those in the synagogue were astounded at the Lord's teaching and said that He taught as One having authority and not as the scribes [Mark 1:22]. The self-appointed scribes, teaching vain knowledge by themselves, had no authority and no power. But this God-authorized Slave, teaching realities by God Himself, had not only spiritual power to subdue people but also divine authority to subject them to the divine ruling. (*Life-study of Mark*, pp. 52-53)

In the Bible, truth refers to the shining of the light. The Bible contains many doctrines. However, when light from the Father in the heavens shines upon the words in the Bible, these words immediately become truth to us. First we have the doctrine in printed letters, and then the heavenly light shines upon words of the Bible to show us the truth. Many read the verses about Christ dying for sinners merely as a newspaper report; they have nothing more than a doctrine about the death of Christ. But when, by the mercy of God, the light shines on these verses, they see the truth of Christ's death and are saved. Once they had the doctrine; now they have the vision and the reality.

There are a great many facts in the Bible. However, it is not adequate merely to read about these facts. By reading you receive doctrine, information, or news. Along with this, you need the heavenly light to shine upon the facts. When the light shines, the doctrine is immediately changed into truth. In this way, you realize the real thing, the reality. Therefore, to know the truth we first need the facts and then the light that "televises" the vision of the facts into our being.

According to the Bible, the Spirit is called the Spirit of truth, the Spirit of reality (John 14:17). The Spirit of reality is the heavenly electricity by which spiritual things are televised into our being. (*Truth Messages*, pp. 18-19)

Further Reading: Truth Messages, chs. 1-2

Enlightenment and inspiration: _____

_____

_____

_____

Morning Nourishment

Mark And He healed many who were ill with various dis-
1:34-35 eases, and He cast out many demons and did not
allow the demons to speak, because they knew Him.
And rising very early in the morning, *while it was
still* night, He went out and went away to a deserted
place, and there He prayed.

1 John ...For this purpose the Son of God was manifested,
3:8 that He might destroy the works of the devil.

The possession of people by demons signifies Satan's usurpation of man, whom God created for His purpose. The Slave-Savior
came to destroy the works of Satan (1 John 3:8), and the third
thing He did as a part of His service to God was to cast out these
demons from the possessed people (Mark 1:34, 39; 3:15; 6:7, 13;
16:17) so that they might be delivered from Satan's bondage (Luke
13:16), out of Satan's authority of darkness (Acts 26:18; Col. 1:13),
into God's kingdom (Mark 1:15). (*Life-study of Mark,* p. 53)

Today's Reading

Mark 1:27 says, "And they were all amazed, so that they
discussed among themselves, saying, What is this? A new
teaching! With authority He orders even the unclean spirits,
and they obey Him." This verse speaks not of the Lord's power,
but of His authority to cast out demons. For His gospel service,
the Slave-Savior had divine authority not only to teach people
(v. 22), but also to cast out demons.

In our preaching of the gospel we should have not only the
proper teaching, but also the casting out of demons, the casting out of those things used by Satan to possess people. In
order to do this, we must learn how to pray to receive the
power, even the authority, to cast out the possessing element.
Once we receive this power and authority, then our preaching
and teaching will come forth with the power to cast out the
possessing element of the enemy.

We need the power to cast out the satanic element used by
the enemy to possess people in today's modern countries.

Satan, the subtle serpent, is very clever, and he knows how to possess people in modern ways. In an uncultured country, he may use an uncultured means to possess people. But in a modern, cultured country, he will use modern, cultured means to usurp people. For example, in the leading colleges and universities, Satan will possess people in an intellectual way. We cannot defeat the enemy's possession of mankind simply by ordinary preaching and teaching. In order to cast out today's demons, in our teaching and preaching we must have divine authority and power. This power and authority can be exercised only in the name of Jesus. Therefore, we need to call on the Lord's name and exercise divine authority in and through His name. If we do this, then in our preaching and teaching there will be power and authority to cast out the evil possessing element of the enemy. The casting out of demons, therefore, is the third item of the content of the gospel.

The fourth thing the Slave-Savior did to rescue sinners, as another part of His gospel service, was to heal their sick condition both physically and spiritually and restore them to normal so that they might serve Him (1:34; 3:10; 6:5, 13, 56).

Today every fallen human being is sick. Many are sick physically, and all are sick spiritually. Because every fallen person is spiritually sick, we in the local churches must learn to preach the gospel and teach the truth like physicians....All the saints among us should learn how to preach the gospel and teach the truth in such a way that people are healed.

Among those in the Pentecostal movement today, a great deal of emphasis is placed on miraculous healing. This emphasis is on physical healing. However, we need to care more for spiritual healing than for physical healing. The church people should be so equipped that in their preaching and teaching spiritual medicine is supplied to people in order that they may be spiritually healed. (*Life-study of Mark*, pp. 53-55)

Further Reading: Life-study of Mark, msgs. 3, 6

Enlightenment and inspiration: _____

_____

_____

_____

Morning Nourishment

Mark
1:40-42

And a leper came to Him, entreating Him and falling on his knees and saying to Him, If You are willing, You can cleanse me. And He was moved with compassion, and stretching out His hand, He touched him and said to him, I am willing; be cleansed! And immediately the leprosy left him, and he was cleansed.

A leper portrays a typical sinner. Leprosy is the most contaminating and damaging disease, much more serious than fever (Mark 1:30), isolating its victim both from God and from men. According to the law, a leper should be excluded from the people because of his uncleanness. No one could touch him (Lev. 13:45-46). According to the scriptural examples, leprosy comes from rebellion and disobedience. Miriam became leprous because of her rebellion against God's deputy authority (Num. 12:1-10). Naaman's leprosy was cleansed because of his obedience (2 Kings 5:1, 9-14). All fallen human beings have become leprous in the sight of God because of their rebellion. Because leprosy isolated its victim from both God and man, to cleanse the leper signifies to recover the sinner to fellowship with God and with men. This was the consummating part of the Slave-Savior's gospel service. (*Life-study of Mark*, p. 56)

Today's Reading

The Slave-Savior's compassion and willingness issuing from His love were dear and precious to the hopeless leper. The Lord stretched out His hand and touched the leper. This showed His sympathy and intimacy with the miserable leper, whom no one dared to touch. According to Mark 1:42, immediately the leprosy left him, and he was cleansed. This verse says that the leper was not only healed, but also cleansed. Leprosy not only requires healing as do other diseases; it also requires cleansing, like sin (1 John 1:7), because of its filthy and contaminating nature.

We all need to be deeply impressed with the five matters comprised in the Slave-Savior's gospel service: preaching (Mark 1:14-15, 38-39) to announce the glad tidings to the miserable people in bondage; teaching (vv. 21-22) to enlighten the ignorant ones in darkness with the divine light of the truth; casting out demons (vv. 25-26) to nullify Satan's usurpation of man; healing man's sick condition (vv. 30-31) that man may serve the Slave-Savior; and cleansing the leper (vv. 41-42) to recover sinners to the fellowship with God and with men. What a wonderful and excellent work!

In our gospel preaching we must also be exercised to preach, teach, cast out demons, heal, and cleanse. If our preaching is weak, some may be saved, but they may not be cleansed. They may be saved in the sense of receiving the forgiveness of sin, but they may not be cleansed from the contaminating nature of sin. Therefore, we need to seriously consider the fact that this picture of the Lord's gospel service concludes with the cleansing of the leper....This cleansing is the ultimate consummation of the contents of the Lord's gospel service. (*Life-study of Mark,* pp. 56-57)

Leprosy may be in a person and also in one's garments. In this message we shall consider the leprosy in a house.

Based upon the principle that Leviticus is written in the form of types, we may interpret the house in 14:33-53 as a type of the church. As New Testament believers, we recognize that our real house is not our physical house but the church. Without the proper church life, we are homeless. Only when we are in the church and live the proper church life are we truly at home. Many have testified upon entering into the church life that they are now at home. The house in Leviticus 14, therefore, typifies the church as our house, our home, and the leprosy in a house signifies sins and evils in the church (vv. 33-48).

Leviticus 14:34 speaks of God's putting a leprous disease in a house of the land of Israel's possession. This signifies that when the condition of a church becomes abnormal, God causes the leprous sin to appear in the church, reminding and warning the believers that they no longer have a house to live in and are no longer able to enjoy all the blessings God promised in His salvation. (*Life-study of Leviticus,* p. 385)

Further Reading: Life-study of Leviticus, msgs. 39-42

Enlightenment and inspiration: _____

_____
_____
_____

Morning Nourishment

Lev. When you come into the land of Canaan, which I
14:34-35 give you for a possession, and I put the infection of
leprosy in a house in the land of your possession,
then he to whom the house belongs shall come and
tell the priest, saying, It seems to me that *there is
something* like an infection in the house.

Heb. How much more will the blood of Christ, who
9:14 through the eternal Spirit offered Himself without
blemish to God, purify our conscience from dead
works to serve the living God?

When the church is sick of leprosy, we lose the enjoyment of
Christ. Since there is no longer a proper church, we are no longer
able to enjoy all the blessings God has promised in His salvation.

[In Leviticus 14:34-35 (above)], the owner's coming and telling
this to the priest signifies that the leading brothers or those who
are concerned for the church approach the Lord or the apostle, the
Lord's deputy, and tell the Lord or His deputy. This is what we
need to do when the church is sick.

"The priest shall command that they empty the house before
the priest goes in to look at the infection, so that everything which
is in the house does not become unclean" (v. 36a). This signifies to
do one's best to prevent and eliminate contagion.

"Afterward the priest shall go in to look at the house" (v. 36b).
This signifies that the Lord or the apostle comes to examine. This
kind of examination is not a matter of condemnation; rather, it is
a kind of grace for healing. (*Life-study of Leviticus,* pp. 386-387)

Today's Reading

When the church is sick of a certain disease, the elders should
first observe the situation. If the problem is becoming worse, the
source of the problem—the believer or believers who have become
involved in the disease—should be removed from the fellowship, the
communication, of the church in order to stop the spread of the disease and to eliminate the disease.

"They shall take other stones and put them in the place of those stones" (v. 42a)....When...[it becomes] necessary to remove...the saints who are involved in the problem,...this will create a gap, and we should seek to fill this gap with other believers.

"And he shall take other plaster and replaster the house" (v. 42b). This is important, for it signifies the renewing of the church with new experiences of the Lord's gracious works.

This is not a matter of simply dealing with a problem but of bringing in the riches of Christ in a new way. If we are unable to do this but simply do something in a legal way to remove certain persons and replace them with others, this will make the church empty, and in this emptiness the church will suffer even more. Therefore, the leading ones need to pray, perhaps with fasting, that the church will receive something new in the experiences of Christ's gracious works. Then the church life will be renewed, replastered with new mortar, and all the members will be happy about the renewed church life.

Leviticus 14:49-51 reveals the leprosy in a house is cleansed in the same way as the cleansing of leprosy in a man....In order for a church to be cleansed, the church needs to experience again the processes through which the Lord Jesus has passed.

"He shall purify the house with the blood of the bird and with the running water..." (v. 52).... The blood of the bird signifies the blood of Christ, the water signifies the cleansing Spirit, and the oil signifies the anointing Spirit. When a church becomes sick, it needs these two elements—the blood of Christ and the Spirit—to recover it.

The more we experience Christ in a new way, the more the church will be healed. A diseased church cannot be healed by discussion, argument, and debate. The more we engage in these things, the more trouble there will be. We need to pray for ourselves and for the church that through the new experiences of Christ, we as members and the church as a whole may have a new start and enter into a new age. (*Life-study of Leviticus*, pp. 388-389, 392-394)

Further Reading: Life-study of Leviticus, msgs. 43-44

Enlightenment and inspiration: _____

_____

_____

_____

Hymns, #559

1 Savior, I by faith am touching
  Thee, the source of every good;
Virtue now, by faith am claiming,
  Through the cleansing of Thy blood.

Touching Thee, new life is glowing
  By Thy Spirit's burning flame;
Cleansing, purging, Spirit filling,
  Glory to Thy Holy Name!

2 Touching Thee in faith, I take Thee
  In Thy riches full and free;
All I am I open to Thee,
  All Thou art Thou giv'st to me.

3 Touching now Thine outstretched scepter,
  O most mighty King of kings;
Of Thy fulness now receiving,
  High I mount on eagle wings.

4 Grace and virtue, strength and wisdom,
  All my need, by Thee supplied;
Keep me touching, keep me claiming,
  Keep me ever at Thy side.

Composition for prophecy with main point and sub-points: _____

_____
_____
_____
_____
_____
_____
_____
_____
_____
_____
_____
_____
_____
_____
_____
_____
_____
_____
_____
_____
_____
_____
_____
_____
_____
_____
_____
_____
_____
_____
_____
_____
_____

The Ways
of the Slave-Savior's Gospel Service

Scripture Reading: Mark 2:1—3:6

Day 1   I. **The five incidents recorded in Mark 2:1—3:6 reveal the five merciful and living ways taken by the Slave-Savior to carry out His gospel service:**

A. As God with divine authority, He forgave the sins of the victim of sickness that He might release him from Satan's oppression (Acts 10:38) and restore him to God; the scribes considered this to be against the theology of their religion (Mark 2:1-12):

   1. The Lord Jesus was both the God-Savior and the Slave-Savior, possessing deity and humanity; He had not only the ability to save sinners but also the authority to forgive their sins (Luke 5:21, 24).

   2. Receiving the forgiveness of our sins causes us to fear God (Psa. 130:4) and to love God (Luke 7:36-50); in the Lord's salvation He not only forgives our sins but also causes us to rise and walk, to "go in peace" (v. 50), and to "go, and from now on sin no more" (John 8:11).

Day 2   B. As a Physician to the sick and miserable people, He feasted with the tax collectors, who were disloyal and unfaithful to their race, and with sinners, who were despised and isolated from society, that they might taste the mercy of God   ·   and be recovered to the enjoyment of God; this was condemned by the self-righteous yet merciless scribes of the Pharisees (Mark 2:13-17):

   1. The self-righteous Pharisees considered themselves strong; hence, blinded by their self-righteousness, they did not know that they were ill and needed Christ as a Physician (Matt. 9:12-13).

2. The Lord as the Physician takes care of His "patients" by causing them to feast with Him, bringing them into the enjoyment of God; the joy of salvation, the enjoyment of God, is a feast (1 Cor. 5:7-8; Psa. 51:2, 12).

Day 3   C. As a Bridegroom with the sons of the bride-chamber, He caused His followers to be merry and happy without fasting; thus, He annulled the practice of the disciples of John (the new religionists) and the Pharisees (the old religionists) so that His followers could be delivered from the practices of their religion into the enjoyment of God's Christ as their Bridegroom, with His righteousness as their outer clothing and His life as their inner wine in God's New Testament economy (Mark 2:18-22):

1. The real meaning of fasting is to stop eating all things other than the Lord Jesus and to not have a taste for anything other than Him (Matt. 6:16-18; Isa. 58:3; John 6:57; cf. Num. 11:4-7).

2. Christ as the Bridegroom gains us to be His overcoming bride as His duplication by being our Physician to organically heal us in our entire tripartite being by His complete salvation (Rom. 5:10; cf. Mal. 4:2):

   a. He is our new cloth as our new garment to clothe us and beautify us with Himself as our God-given righteousness through the shedding of His precious blood applied to us for our judicial redemption (Luke 15:22; 1 Cor. 1:30; Matt. 9:16).

   b. He is our new wine as our new life to fill us and cheer us with Himself as our God-given portion through the dispensing of His priceless life into us for our organic salvation (Judg. 9:13; Matt. 9:17; Col. 1:12).

3. We are not only the bride of Christ but also "the sons of the bridechamber" (Mark 2:19)

to be the corporate "best man" of Christ as the Bridegroom; by enjoying Him as our new garment and new wine, we become His corporate "best man," the Body of Christ as the new man.

Day 4 D. The Lord allowed His followers to pick the ears of grain in the grainfields on the Sabbath so that they could satisfy their hunger; thus, apparently they broke God's commandment concerning the Sabbath, but actually they pleased God because the hunger of Christ's followers was satisfied through Him, as the hunger of David and his followers had been satisfied with the bread of the Presence in the house of God; this indicates that in God's New Testament economy, it is a matter not of keeping the regulation of religion but of enjoying satisfaction in and through Christ as the real Sabbath rest (vv. 23-28):

1. The real meaning of keeping the Sabbath is that we cease from our doing, stop our work, and enjoy what the Lord has done for us by eating Him as the bread of the Presence for our nourishment and supply (Exo. 25:30).

2. Man was not created for the Sabbath, but the Sabbath was ordained for man so that he might enjoy it with God; God first worked and then rested; man first rests and then works (Gen. 2:2-3).

3. Keeping the Sabbath is a sign that God's people work for God not by their own strength but by enjoying Him and being filled with Him to be one with Him; it is also an eternal covenant assuring God that we will be one with Him by first enjoying Him and then working with Him (Exo. 31:12-17).

Day 5 E. On the Sabbath the Lord healed a man who had a withered hand, caring not for the keeping of the Sabbath but for the health of His sheep; thus

He indicated that in God's New Testament economy it is a matter not of keeping regulations but of imparting life (Mark 3:1-6):

1. This is the case of a person who is partially free but not wholly free; like the man with the withered hand, we need to be fully liberated.

2. The Slave-Savior is our Emancipator, setting us free from religious ritual and from the slavery of sin; we may be liberated to a certain extent, but in certain parts of our life we still need to be freed by the Slave-Savior (John 8:32, 36; Rom. 6:12-23; 8:2).

Day 6 II. **The above five ways of the Slave-Savior's gospel service can be summarized by five words: *forgiveness* (Mark 2:1-12), *enjoyment* (vv. 13-17), *joy* (vv. 18-22), *satisfaction* (vv. 23-28), and *freedom* (3:1-6); we can experience Him as our full salvation in all these aspects by touching Him (5:24-34):**

A. When we contact the Lord directly, having a direct touch with Him, He is transfused into us as the power of God to become our healing; the genuine way to help people is to bring them into a direct touch with the Lord.

B. We all have to contact the Lord, to fellowship with Him, and to touch Him moment by moment in our spirit so that He can be our daily salvation and moment-by-moment supply for the building up of His Body (John 4:24).

Morning Nourishment

Mark
2:5

And Jesus, seeing their faith, said to the paralytic, Child, your sins are forgiven.

8-11

And immediately Jesus, knowing fully in His spirit that they were reasoning this way within themselves, said to them, Why are you reasoning about these things in your hearts? Which is easier: to say to the paralytic, Your sins are forgiven, or to say, Rise and take up your mat and walk? But that you may know that the Son of Man has authority to forgive sins on earth—He said to the paralytic, To you I say, Rise, take up your mat and go to your house.

The five incidents recorded vividly in Mark 2:1—3:6 form one particular group, showing how the Slave-Savior as the Slave of God carried out His gospel service to care for the need of fallen people, who were captured by Satan from God and the enjoyment of God. The Lord cared for their need so that they might be rescued from their captivity and brought back to the God of enjoyment.

First, the Lord forgave the sins of the victim of sickness. He did this as God with divine authority so that He might release the sick one from Satan's oppression (Acts 10:38) and restore him to God. The scribes considered this to be against the theology of their religion (2:1-12). (*Life-study of Mark,* p. 60)

Today's Reading

The Gospel of Mark...presents the Lord in the likeness of man and in the form of a slave. The scribes did not realize that within the humanity of this Slave there was deity. The Lord behaved Himself in such a way as to indicate that within His humanity there was deity. The Lord was a Nazarene in the form of a slave; yet He had omniscience. Because He was omniscient, He knew what the scribes were saying in their hearts [Mark 2:8].

The Slave-Savior was the very God incarnated....Hence, He had not only the ability to save the sinners, but also the authority to forgive their sins [Mark 2:10-11]. In this incident He forgave people's sins as God, but asserted that He was the Son of Man.

This indicates that He was the true God and a real Man, possessing deity and humanity. In Him men could see both His divine attribute and human virtue.

These verses indicate that in order to show that He had authority to forgive sins, the Lord said to the paralytic, "Rise, take up your mat and go to your house." This was the healing of the paralytic. The Lord's salvation not only forgives our sins, but also makes us "rise and walk." It is not rise and walk first, and then be forgiven of our sins; that would be by works. Instead, it is to be forgiven of our sins first, and then to rise and walk; this is by grace. (*Life-study of Mark,* pp. 66-67)

People think that God's forgiveness will cause man to become audacious and reckless. Little do they know that the grace of God's forgiveness is to bring man into the fear of God (Psa. 130:4)....Once we have tasted the grace of God's forgiveness, we immediately have a fearful heart and we also hate sin.

The grace of God's forgiveness causes us not only to fear God but also to love God. On the negative side, because we fear Him, we refrain from doing things that are displeasing to God; on the positive side, because we love Him, we do things that are pleasing to Him....In Luke 7, the sinful woman, having been forgiven by the Lord, not only ceased from her sinful living but also poured out all she had and all she was on the Lord to express her love toward Him. The law, which condemns us, cannot free us from sin, but grace, which forgives us, can. The condemnation at Mount Sinai could cause man only to be afraid of God and go far away from Him, but the forgiveness at the mount of Golgotha causes man to love God and draw near to Him. The more we have been forgiven by God, the more we love God. The reason that sinful woman loved the Lord much was that she was forgiven much by the Lord. Therefore, God's forgiveness of man results in man's fearing Him and loving Him. (*Truth Lessons, Level One,* vol. 3, pp. 130-131)

Further Reading: Life-study of Mark, msg. 7; *Truth Lessons, Level One,* vol. 3, lsn. 36

Enlightenment and inspiration: _____

_____

_____

_____

Morning Nourishment

Mark
2:15-17

And as He reclined *at table* in his house, many tax collectors and sinners were reclining together with Jesus and His disciples, for there were many, and they were following Him. And the scribes of the Pharisees, seeing that He ate with sinners and tax collectors, said to His disciples, Why does He eat with tax collectors and sinners? And when Jesus heard *this*, He said to them, Those who are strong have no need of a physician, but those who are ill; I did not come to call the righteous, but sinners.

As a physician to the sick and miserable people, [the Lord] feasted with the tax collectors, those who were disloyal and unfaithful to their race, and with sinners despised and isolated from society, that they might taste the mercy of God and be recovered to the enjoyment of God. This was condemned by the self-righteous yet merciless scribes of the Pharisees (Mark 2:13-17). (*Life-study of Mark*, p. 60)

Today's Reading

In calling people to follow Him, the Lord ministered as a Physician [Mark 2:17], not as a judge. The judgment of a judge is according to righteousness, whereas the healing of a physician is according to mercy and grace. The Lord came to minister as a Physician; that is, He came to heal, recover, enliven, and save people.

The Lord's word that the strong have no need of a physician implies that the self-righteous scribes did not realize their need of Him as a Physician. They considered themselves strong. Therefore, blinded by their self-righteousness, they did not know that they were sick.

In verse 17 the Lord said that He did not come to call the righteous, but sinners. This indicates that the Slave-Savior is the Savior of sinners. Actually, there is none righteous, not even one (Rom. 3:10). Those who think they are righteous are self-righteous. The Slave-Savior did not come to call these "righteous" ones; He came to call sinners.

[In the Lord's] forgiving the sins of the sick and feasting with sinners, we see the best way to carry out the gospel service. This is to help people have their sins forgiven so that they may enter into the enjoyment with God. To feast with the Lord Jesus is to enjoy God with Him.

All sinners have lost God and have also lost the enjoyment of God. Sinners have been taken captive away from God and from the enjoyment of God to be slaves of Satan....Because they are such slaves, they have no enjoyment and no peace. In carrying out the service of the gospel, the Lord Jesus first forgives our sins and then brings us into the enjoyment of God.

After you were saved, did you not experience an enjoyment that could be compared to a feast? If you were saved without having such a feast, this means that you did not have the joy of God's salvation. In this sense, your experience of salvation was not adequate, not complete. Complete salvation includes forgiveness of sins and a joy that is in God. This joy is the enjoyment of God, and this enjoyment is a feast.

The joy of salvation is a feast. When we have the joy of salvation, we are feasting with the Lord Jesus. Many of us can testify that when we recall our experience of salvation, we can still taste the joy we experienced. After we were saved and knew that our sins had been forgiven, there was joy within us. We regarded the Lord Jesus as the most wonderful One, and we were joyful in Him, feasting with Him.

This joy of salvation, the enjoyment of God, is a strong proof that we have been brought back to God. The joy of salvation testifies that we are no longer far away from God but have been brought back to Him. The proper way to carry out the gospel service is to help people experience the forgiveness of sins so that they may have the joy of salvation, the enjoyment of God. (*Life-study of Mark,* pp. 74-75)

Further Reading: Life-study of Mark, msg. 8; *Life-study of Matthew,* msg. 27

Enlightenment and inspiration: _____

_____

_____

_____

Morning Nourishment

Mark   And the disciples of John and the Pharisees were fast-
2:18-19 ing. And they came and said to Him, Why do the disci-
        ples of John and the disciples of the Pharisees fast, but
        Your disciples do not fast? And Jesus said to them, The
        sons of the bridechamber cannot fast while the bride-
        groom is with them, can they? For as long a time as
        they have the bridegroom with them they cannot fast.
21-22   No one sews a patch of unfulled cloth on an old gar-
        ment; otherwise, that which fills it up pulls away
        from it, the new from the old, and a worse tear is
        made. And no one puts new wine into old wineskins;
        otherwise, the wine will burst the wineskins, and the
        wine is ruined as well as the wineskins; but new wine
        is put into fresh wineskins.

[The Lord] caused His followers to be merry and happy
without fasting, as a bridegroom with the sons of the bridechamber. Thus, He annulled the practice of the disciples of John
(the new religionists) and the Pharisees (the old religionists), so
that His followers might be delivered from the practices of their
religion into the enjoyment of God's Christ as their Bridegroom,
with His righteousness as their outer clothing and His life as
their inner wine in God's New Testament economy (Mark 2:18-
22). (*Life-study of Mark*, p. 60)

Today's Reading

The real meaning of fasting is to stop eating all things other
than the Lord Jesus and to not have a taste for anything other
than Him. God wants us to stop our doing and be replaced by
Christ (keep the Sabbath—Isa. 56:2) and to keep away from the
taste of anything other than Christ (fast). By resting and fasting
we can partake of all that the processed Christ has accomplished
for us. (Isa. 58:3, footnote 1)

Those in religion certainly have reason to fast. Religion
requires and demands....However, religion does not enable us to
fulfill its requirements. Because those in a religion cannot fulfill

the requirements of their religion, they need to fast. Therefore, [in Mark 2] both the disciples of John and the disciples of the Pharisees were fasting.

In contrast,…the Lord's disciples were full of joy. How could they fast when the Bridegroom, the most important factor of their joy, was with them? In Mark 2:19…the Lord refers to His disciples as sons of the bridechamber. For them to fast when the Bridegroom is with them would be a shame to Him.

The Lord answered the disciples of John and the Pharisees not in a direct way but by using certain figures of speech. In His answer the Lord referred to Himself as the Bridegroom, and He also spoke of new cloth and new wine. The Lord seemed to be saying, "Why should My disciples fast when they have everything they need to make them joyful? They have Me as the Bridegroom, and they have Me as their righteousness, their new cloth, and also as their life, their new wine. I am everything they need. I am God and Man; I am the Physician and the Bridegroom, the most pleasant person. It is ridiculous for My disciples to fast when they have Me. I am the garment that covers them and beautifies them, and My life is the real wine that fills them, stirs them, and satisfies them. Instead of fasting, they should be full of joy. You ask them to fast. But I tell you it is impossible for them to fast, because the Bridegroom is here with them, the new cloth is upon them, and the new wine is within them." How wise and how wonderful is the Lord's answer, His word concerning the Bridegroom, the cloth, and wine!

We should…tell…people that Jesus Christ today is the Bridegroom, that He as our righteousness is the cloth to cover our nakedness and to beautify us, and that His divine life is the wine for us to drink for our satisfaction. This is the real gospel—a living Person with righteousness and life. Hallelujah, we have the Bridegroom, and we have Him as righteousness outwardly and as our life inwardly! (*Life-study of Mark,* pp. 83-86)

Further Reading: Life-study of Mark, msg. 7; *Life-study of Matthew,* msg. 28

Enlightenment and inspiration: _____

_____

_____

_____

Morning Nourishment

Mark 2:25-28

And He said to them, Have you never read what David did when he had need and became hungry, he and those with him; how he entered into the house of God during the time of Abiathar the high priest and ate the bread of the Presence, which is not lawful *for anyone* to eat except the priests, and he gave also to those who were with him? And He said to them, The Sabbath came into being for man, and not man for the Sabbath. So then the Son of Man is Lord even of the Sabbath.

[The Lord] allowed His followers to pick the ears of grain in the grainfields on the Sabbath that they might satisfy their hunger. Thus, they apparently broke God's commandment concerning the Sabbath. But actually they pleased God, for the hunger of Christ's followers was satisfied through Him, as the hunger of David and his followers was satisfied with the bread of the Presence in the temple. This indicates that in God's New Testament economy it is not a matter of keeping the regulation of religion, but of enjoying satisfaction in and through Christ as the real Sabbath rest (Mark 2:23-28). (*Life-study of Mark*, pp. 60-61)

Today's Reading

The Lord Jesus indicated to the condemning Pharisees that He was the real David, the King of the coming kingdom of God, and also the Lord of the Sabbath. Therefore, He could do whatever He liked on the Sabbath, and whatever He did was justified by who He is. He was above all rituals and regulations. Because He was present, no one should pay any attention to rituals and regulations.

[In Mark 2:28] the Lord says that the Son of Man is the Lord *even* of the Sabbath. His use of the word "even" here implies that He is not merely the Lord of one thing, but the Lord of everything, including the Sabbath. The Lord's word implies and indicates that He is the almighty God, the very One who ordained the Sabbath in Genesis 2. As the One who had the authority to ordain the Sabbath, He also has the right to change it. (*Life-study of Mark*, p. 92)

When God saw the man created by Him [Gen. 1:26-28], He could rest [2:2-3] and be refreshed. Man was like a refreshing drink to quench God's thirst and satisfy Him. When God ended His work and began to rest, He had man as His companion. To God, the seventh day was a day of rest and refreshment. However, to man, God's companion, the day of rest and refreshment was the first day. Man's first day was a day of enjoyment.

It is a divine principle that God does not ask us to work until we have had enjoyment. God first supplies us with enjoyment. Then after a full enjoyment with Him and of Him, we may work together with Him. If we do not know how to have enjoyment with God and how to enjoy God Himself, we shall not know how to work with Him. We shall not know how to be one with God in His divine work.

We have emphasized that to God the Sabbath is the seventh day and to man, the first day; that God worked for man's enjoyment and rest; and that man enjoys what God has accomplished in His work in order to work with God. Man in his first day enjoyed what God accomplished in the previous six days. Then in the following six days man worked with God. After six days' work, man again first enjoyed what God had accomplished, and then he worked again the following six days. This proceeds as a cycle. This cycle is a sign that we are one with God.

Keeping the Sabbath is also an agreement or covenant. When we begin to keep the Sabbath, this indicates that we have signed an agreement, a contract, that assures God that we shall be one with Him in this way. We would be one with Him by first enjoying Him and then by working for Him, with Him, and in oneness with Him. This is an eternal covenant. It is not merely for one age, dispensation, or generation. It is an eternal agreement between us and God. (*Life-study of Exodus*, pp. 1824, 1828)

Further Reading: Life-study of Mark, msg. 10, pp. 89-93; *Life-study of Exodus*, msg. 172

Enlightenment and inspiration: _____

_____

_____

_____

Morning Nourishment

Mark
3:2-5

And they were watching Him closely *to see* if He would heal him on the Sabbath, so that they might accuse Him. And He said to the man who had the withered hand, Rise *and stand* in the midst. And He said to them, Is it lawful on the Sabbath to do good or to do evil, to save life or to kill? But they remained silent. And looking around at them with anger and being greatly grieved with the hardness of their heart, He said to the man, Stretch out your hand. And he stretched *it* out, and his hand was restored.

The Lord healed a man with a withered hand on the Sabbath. He did not care for keeping the Sabbath, but rather cared for the health of His sheep. Thus, He indicated that in God's New Testament economy it is not a matter of keeping regulations but of imparting life. For this, He was hated by the Pharisees—the religionists (Mark 3:1-6).

All the five merciful and living ways taken by the Slave-Savior to carry out His gospel service contradicted the formal and traditional religion and were thus abhorred by its fleshly and stubborn leaders, who were spiritually dead. (*Life-study of Mark,* p. 61)

Today's Reading

Mark 2:23—3:6 records the Lord's move on two Sabbaths (Luke 6:1, 6). What He did on the first Sabbath indicates that He was acting as the Head of the Body. As the Head, He is the real David and the Lord of the Sabbath. What He did on the second Sabbath signifies that He cared for His members. On this Sabbath He healed a man's withered hand. The hand is a member of the body. The Lord would do anything for the healing of His members. Sabbath or no Sabbath, the Lord is interested in healing the members of His Body who are in need, even healing the members who are dead. Regulations do not matter, but the healing of the members of His Body means everything to Him.

In these two portions we have two cases of the breaking of the Sabbath. The first instance of breaking the Sabbath took place in the grainfields; the second took place in a synagogue (3:1). The first breaking of the Sabbath was related to satisfaction, and the second was related to liberation.

According to the sequence in the Gospel of Mark, liberation follows satisfaction. If we have not been satisfied, we shall not sense the need for liberation. Our immediate need is to have our hunger satisfied. First, the Lord satisfies our hunger, and then... He heals us and we are liberated.

In 3:4 the Lord said to those in the synagogue, "Is it lawful on the Sabbath to do good or to do evil, to save life or to kill?" This word implies that the Slave-Savior was the Emancipator, who set the suffering one free from the bondage of religious ritual.

In 2:1-12 we have the case of a paralytic, the case of someone fully paralyzed. But in 3:1-6 we have the case of someone with a withered hand. This is the case of a person who is partially free, but is not wholly free. Are you fully free? You may...say, "On the one hand, I cannot say that I am wholly free. On the other hand, it would not be true to say that I am not free at all. I must answer by saying that I am partially free." Like the man with the withered hand, we need to be fully liberated. This man was not dying. He could move about and do things with one of his hands. Yet the other hand was withered. This indicates that he needed to be set free.

It is significant that the case of the man with the withered hand is the last of the five cases in 2:1—3:6. In the first incident (2:1-12) we have the forgiveness of sins; in the second (2:13-17), the entering into the enjoyment of God; in the third (2:18-22), joy through the living Christ as the Bridegroom, the One who has a garment with which to cover and beautify us and who has the divine life with which to fill us; and in the fourth (2:23-28), satisfaction through the Lord's feeding. Now in the fifth incident we have complete freedom. Here we see a person who is wholly free. (*Life-study of Mark,* pp. 93-95)

Further Reading: Life-study of Mark, msg. 10, pp. 93-96; *Life-study of Matthew,* msg. 32

Enlightenment and inspiration: _____

_____

_____

_____

Morning Nourishment

Mark When she heard the things concerning Jesus, she
5:27-29 came up in the crowd behind *Him* and touched His
garment, for she said, If I touch even His garments,
I will be healed. And immediately the fountain of
her blood was dried up, and she knew in her body
that she was cured of the affliction.
34 And He said to her, Daughter, your faith has healed
you. Go in peace and be well from your affliction.

We have seen that the five incidents recorded in Mark 2:1—
3:6 form a group....The word to summarize the first incident is
forgiveness. In 2:1-12 we have a case of the forgiveness of sins by
the Son of Man, who was the forgiving God incarnated in the form
of a Slave.

The word to describe the second incident is enjoyment. In this
incident, recorded in 2:13-17, the Slave-Savior as a Physician was
feasting with sinners.

We may use a very simple word to describe the third incident—joy [2:18-22]....We can be joyful because we are with the
Bridegroom, because we have a new covering to beautify us, and
because we have new wine to fill us, satisfy us, and cause us to be
beside ourselves with joy.

The fourth incident...[2:23-28] is that of the Lord's caring for
His followers' hunger rather than for religion's regulation.

The word that best summarizes the fifth incident, that of the
Slave-Savior's caring for the relief of the suffering one rather than
for the ritual of religion (3:1-6), is the word freedom. In this incident we see that on the Sabbath the Savior restored a man's withered hand. (*Life-study of Mark*, pp. 79-81)

Today's Reading

[In Mark 3:7-12] the crowd's pressing hindered the way for the
sincere ones to come to the Lord and touch Him directly. If we are
among those who merely press upon the Lord, we shall not
receive anything from Him. In order to receive from Him, we need
to touch Him. Therefore, in this portion of the Gospel of Mark the

word "press" is used in a negative sense, whereas the word "touch" has a positive meaning.

A number of times people pressed upon the Lord. But only those who touched Him received any benefit. It is through a direct touch with the Lord that life is imparted from Him to us....Pressing upon the Lord does not accomplish anything as far as the divine dispensing is concerned. We experience the divine dispensing only by directly touching the Lord.

Although the Lord sought to avoid the crowd, He wanted the sincere ones to be able to touch Him. If we are simply part of the crowd, we shall not receive anything from the Lord. We need to single ourselves out from among the crowd and touch Him directly and honestly. If we do this, we shall receive the ministry of life.

When a crowd surrounds us, this may be deceiving; it also may be frustrating. Hence, we need to avoid the crowd. But this does not mean that we should give up the people. No, as we avoid the crowd, we need to allow others to contact us, to touch us, directly in order to receive the genuine ministry of life.

[In Mark 5:28-29], because a crowd was pressing upon the Slave-Savior, it was difficult for the genuine seekers to touch Him. Nevertheless, this woman found a way to touch Him, and when she did so, she was healed. "And immediately Jesus, realizing in Himself that power had gone out of Him, turned around in the crowd and said, Who touched My garments?" (v. 30). The Lord had the inner sense that His virtue, His power, had gone out of Him and had been transfused into someone else. This was the reason He asked who it was that had touched His garments. The disciples, being natural and seeing the crowd pressing upon Him, said, "You see the crowd pressing upon You and You say, Who touched Me?" (v. 31). The pressing crowd received nothing from the Savior, but the woman who touched Him was healed. (*Life-study of Mark,* pp. 98-100, 156-157)

Further Reading: Life-study of Mark, msgs. 11, 17; *Perfecting Training,* ch. 33

Enlightenment and inspiration: _____

_____

_____

_____

Hymns, #310

1   Once I was bound by sin's galling fetters,
Chained like a slave I struggled in vain;
But I received a glorious freedom,
When Jesus broke my fetters in twain.

Glorious freedom, wonderful freedom,
No more in chains of sin I repine!
Jesus the glorious Emancipator,
Now and forever He shall be mine.

2   Freedom from all the carnal affections,
Freedom from envy, hatred and strife;
Freedom from vain and worldly ambitions.
Freedom from all that saddened my life.

3   Freedom from pride and all sinful follies,
Freedom from love and glitter of gold;
Freedom from evil temper and anger,
Glorious freedom, rapture untold.

4   Freedom from fear with all of its torments,
Freedom from care with all of its pain;
Freedom in Christ my blessed Redeemer,
He who has rent my fetters in twain.

Composition for prophecy with main point and sub-points: _____

_____
_____
_____
_____
_____
_____
_____
_____
_____
_____
_____
_____
_____
_____
_____
_____
_____
_____
_____
_____
_____
_____
_____
_____
_____
_____
_____
_____
_____
_____
_____
_____
_____
_____
_____
_____

A Life Fully according to and for God's New Testament Economy (1)

Scripture Reading: Mark 1:1-11, 35; 10:45

Day 1   I. In the Gospel of Mark we see a person, the
God-man, who lived a life that was fully
according to and for God's New Testament
economy; the Lord's life was His work, and
His work was His move; His work was His
living and His move was His being (Mark
1:35; 10:45; cf. John 6:38; 4:34):

A. The Lord Jesus lived in a new dispensation,
having the old dispensation terminated; the
New Testament dispensation, the dispensation
of grace, that is, the dispensation of the gospel of
Jesus Christ, began from the preaching of John
the Baptist (Mark 1:1-8; Matt. 11:13; Luke
16:16; Acts 10:37):

1. Instead of serving with his father Zacha-
riah in the temple, John stayed in a wild
place, wore wild clothing, ate wild food, and
did a wild work; where he lived, what he
wore, what he ate, and how he worked
ended the Old Testament priesthood; his
work was the beginning of the priesthood
in the New Testament (Mark 1:1-8).

2. The first New Testament priest of the
gospel of God was John the Baptist; he
did not offer bulls and goats as sacrifices
(Heb. 10:1-4), but he offered sinners saved
through his preaching as sacrifices, bringing them to Christ as the One stronger than
he was and as the One baptizing the repentant people in the Holy Spirit for imparting
life (Mark 1:4-8).

3. In the New Testament the saved sinners
are spiritual sacrifices offered to God in
Christ, with Christ, and one with Christ as

members of Christ, the enlargement and increase of Christ (Rom. 15:16; 1 Pet. 2:5, 9).

Day 2 B. When the Lord Jesus was about to begin His ministry, He had Himself buried, baptized, by John the Baptist (Mark 1:9-11):

1. John came in "the way of righteousness" (Matt. 21:32); to repent and be baptized according to John's preaching and practice was ordained by God according to the righteous requirements of God's eternal economy; hence, it is to fulfill the righteousness of God as a matter of eternity (2 Pet. 3:13).

2. As a man in the flesh (John 1:14; Rom. 8:3), the Lord recognized that He needed to be a dead man buried in the death water to fulfill God's New Testament requirement according to His righteousness, and He did it willingly, considering it as the fulfilling of God's righteousness (Matt. 3:15).

3. By His baptism He declared to the whole universe that He did not depend at all upon the flesh for God's ministry; instead, He rejected Himself, put Himself aside, in order to live by God; this is the intrinsic significance of the base of Jesus' baptism.

4. We all should declare in our life and work: "I am a person in the flesh, worthy of nothing in the eyes of God but death and burial; so I want to have myself terminated, crucified and buried."

Day 3 C. Immediately after His baptism the Lord Jesus was thrust into the wilderness by the Holy Spirit (Mark 1:12-13); from that time onward He fulfilled His ministry by living, moving, and working in the Holy Spirit:

1. He preached the gospel (vv. 14-20), taught the truth (vv. 21-22), cast out demons (vv. 23-28), healed the sick (vv. 29-39), and cleansed the leper (vv. 40-45); the result of

such a life, fully according to and for God's New Testament economy, was for people to experience the Lord as their forgiveness (2:1-12), enjoyment (vv. 13-17), joy (vv. 18-22), satisfaction (vv. 23-28), and freedom (3:1-6).

2. While the Lord Jesus was carrying out such a gospel service, He was also binding Satan and plundering his kingdom (vv. 22-30), denying any natural relationship (vv. 31-35), suffering the world's rejection and hatred (6:1-6), and exposing man's inward evil condition (7:1-23).

3. Then He presented Himself as the bread of life to be the life supply to His seeking one (vv. 24-30).

4. He healed the hearing, speaking, and seeing organs of the enlivened ones (vv. 31-37; 8:22-26).

5. He revealed Himself as our universal and entire replacement through His all-inclusive death and wonderful resurrection (8:27—9:13).

6. He accomplished an all-inclusive death to bear our sins (1 Pet. 2:24; 1 Cor. 15:3), condemn sin (2 Cor. 5:21; Rom. 8:3), crucify the old man (6:6; Gal. 2:20), terminate the old creation (Col. 1:15; Exo. 26:31; Matt. 27:51), destroy Satan (Heb. 2:14), judge the world (John 12:31), abolish the ordinances (Eph. 2:15), and release the divine life (John 12:24; 19:34).

Day 4

7. He then entered into His wonderful resurrection to regenerate His followers and germinate the new creation (1 Pet. 1:3; 2 Cor. 5:17).

8. After His resurrection the Lord Jesus "was taken up into heaven and sat at the right hand of God" (Mark 16:19); He now remains in His ascension to execute what He has

accomplished through His death and resurrection.

9. By bringing His followers into His death, resurrection, and ascension (Gal. 2:20; Eph. 2:6), He brought forth the new man (v. 15) as the reality of the kingdom of God, issuing in the church, developing into the millennium, and consummating in the New Jerusalem in the new heaven and new earth; this will be our eternal destiny, and this is also the conclusion of the Scriptures (Rev. 21:9—22:5).

Day 5
&
Day 6

II. **The Gospel of Mark conveys a heavenly vision of a life that lives and expresses God as a complete, whole, perfect, and entire pattern of God's New Testament economy; this governing vision directs our steps, controls our living, and brings us into God's consummation (Prov. 29:18a; Acts 26:19):**

A. The life that the Lord Jesus lived is now our life; today we are His expansion, increase, and continuation, and we should continue to live the kind of life He lived; God has put us into Christ that we may live a life of Christ to carry out His New Testament economy (1 Cor. 1:30; Gal. 2:20).

B. This life indwelling our spirit is a law that automatically lives and expresses Christ to produce the Body; any other way of living is a factor of division that damages the Body (Rom. 8:2, 6, 10-11; Gal. 5:22; Eph. 4:3-6).

C. The life we live today should be Christ Himself; only a life that is Christ is fully according to and for God's New Testament economy (Col. 3:4; Phil. 1:21a).

Morning Nourishment

Mark
1:1-6

The beginning of the gospel of Jesus Christ, the Son of God, even as it is written in Isaiah the prophet: "Behold, I send My messenger before Your face, who will prepare Your way, a voice of one crying in the wilderness: Prepare the way of the Lord; make straight His paths." John came baptizing in the wilderness and preaching a baptism of repentance for forgiveness of sins. And all the region of Judea went out to him, and all the *people* of Jerusalem; and they were baptized by him in the Jordan River, as they confessed their sins. And John was clothed in camel's hair and *had* a leather girdle around his loins, and he ate locusts and wild honey.

The entire New Testament is the dispensation of grace, which is the dispensation of the gospel of Jesus Christ. This dispensation began from the preaching of John the Baptist. This is proved by Mark 1:1-4....John's coming out to preach his gospel was counted as the beginning of the gospel of Jesus Christ. (*The God-man Living,* pp. 45-46)

Today's Reading

In John the Baptist, we see the turn of the priesthood from the Old Testament to the New Testament....In the eyes of God, the Old Testament priesthood lasted until John the Baptist. John's work indicated that he did not want anything to do with the holy temple, the holy clothing, the holy diet, and the holy sacrifices of the Old Testament. The Old Testament priests handled the offerings, washed at the laver, and entered the Holy Place to arrange the showbread, tend the lampstand, and burn the incense before God at the incense altar. This service was very cultured and religious, but John the Baptist gave this up. With him there was no culture or religion. Everything was new with him. Where he lived, what he wore, what he ate, and how he worked ended the Old Testament priesthood.

John the Baptist denied the entire Old Testament priesthood, but his work was the beginning of the priesthood in the New Testament (Mark 1:1-4). He preached the baptism of repentance for forgiveness of sins as the gospel of Jesus Christ. His ministry was "the beginning of the gospel of Jesus Christ, the Son of God" (Mark 1:1). He did not offer bulls and goats as sacrifices (Heb. 10:1-4), but he offered sinners saved through his preaching as sacrifices (Mark 1:5). John the Baptist brought people to Christ as the One stronger than he was and as the One baptizing the repentant people in the Holy Spirit for imparting life (Mark 1:7-8). The first New Testament priest of the gospel of God was John the Baptist, the forerunner of the Lord Jesus. He was the ending of the Old Testament priesthood and the beginning of the New Testament priesthood. From the time of John the Baptist, the priesthood is no longer busy with animal sacrifices. From that time on, the New Testament priesthood is busy with the preaching of the gospel of Jesus Christ, which is the gospel of God.

The book of Romans shows us that the preaching of the gospel is not merely the winning of souls. When we preach the gospel we make sinners the sons of God and the members of Christ, and we help them to grow so that they can be the active members in the practice of the Body life. Whatever Paul did was his service in the gospel:..."For God is my witness, whom I serve in my spirit in the gospel of His Son" [Rom. 1:9]. The preaching of the gospel of God is the very service we should render to God in our spirit. To serve God is to handle the gospel, and to handle the gospel is to preach the gospel in order that Christ might be imparted to others, dispensed to others, that others might become the members of Christ, that Christ's Body might be constituted, and that many local churches could be raised up for His Body to be expressed in many localities. This is the preaching of the gospel, and this is the New Testament service, which is called the New Testament priesthood. (*The Advance of the Lord's Recovery Today,* pp. 15-16, 21-22)

Further Reading: The God-man Living, msg. 5; *The Advance of the Lord's Recovery Today,* ch. 1; *Life-study of Mark,* msg. 55

Enlightenment and inspiration: _____

_____

_____

_____

Morning Nourishment

Mark   I have baptized you in water, but He Himself will bap-
1:8   tize you in the Holy Spirit.
Matt. Then Jesus came from Galilee to the Jordan to John
3:13-15 to be baptized by him. But John tried to prevent Him,
       saying, *It is* I *who* have need of being baptized by You,
       and You come to me? But Jesus answered and said to
       him, Permit it for now, for it is fitting for us in this way
       to fulfill all righteousness. Then he permitted Him.

John came in the way of righteousness and preached, "Repent,
for the kingdom of the heavens has drawn near" (Matt. 3:2). The
Israelites who were under the ministry of the law of Moses
needed to repent because they were all practicing unrighteous-
ness. The record of the society of Israel in Isaiah 1 shows how evil
the people had become. The evils seen in Gentile society could
also be seen in Israel's society.

John charged the people to repent because of the kingdom
of the heavens. The kingdom of God is of righteousness (Rom.
14:17), and the kingdom of the heavens is particularly based upon
righteousness. In Matthew 5:20 the Lord said, "Unless your righteousness surpasses that of the scribes and Pharisees, you shall by
no means enter into the kingdom of the heavens." This righteousness is the foundation of God's throne (Psa. 89:14). (*The God-man
Living*, p. 46)

Today's Reading

The people received John's preaching and came to repent to
him....Perhaps some people thought that there should be a good
result after their repenting to John. Instead, John put them into
the water to bury them, indicating that they were good for nothing [Rom. 7:18]. I believe this was why the Pharisees and Saddu-
cees would not come to John.

The first thought of the New Testament dispensation of grace,
the dispensation of the gospel of Jesus Christ, is that all fallen
men of the flesh are worthy of nothing except death and burial.
This is very serious.

Thus, to repent and be baptized according to John's preaching and practice was ordained by God according to the righteous requirements of God's eternal economy; hence, it is to fulfill the righteousness of God (Matt. 3:15) as a matter of eternity. To be baptized is to keep God's New Testament ordinance, to recognize yourself before God according to His evaluation, and to fulfill God's righteous requirement.

The base for Jesus to be baptized is that He considered Himself, according to His humanity, a man, especially an Israelite, who is a man "in the flesh" (John 1:14). Even though He was only "in the likeness of the flesh of sin" (Rom. 8:3), "without sin" (Heb. 4:15), yet He was "in the flesh," which has nothing good but is worthy only of death and burial....He was standing on that ground, and that ground became His base for Him to be baptized.

As a man in the flesh, He needed to be a dead man buried in the death water to fulfill God's New Testament requirement according to His righteousness, and He did it willingly, considering it the fulfilling of God's righteousness. Such a base surely is proper and righteous.

Before the Lord Jesus began to do anything for His ministry, the first thing He did was to come to John to receive such a baptism to declare to the whole universe that He did not depend at all upon the flesh for God's ministry. We all have to see this. No one should bring anything of his natural life, anything of his flesh, into God's ministry. Especially the co-workers and elders need to realize that as a natural man in the flesh, we are good for nothing except death and burial. We need to have ourselves absolutely terminated in the water of baptism. This is the intrinsic significance of the base of Jesus' baptism....We all should declare in our life and work: "I am a person in the flesh, worthy of nothing in the eyes of God but death and burial; so I want to have myself terminated, crucified and buried." (*The God-man Living,* pp. 46-47, 49-50, 53)

Further Reading: The God-man Living, msgs. 5-6; *Life-study of Mark,* msg. 56

Enlightenment and inspiration: _____

Morning Nourishment

Mark **And immediately the Spirit thrust Him out into**
1:12-13 **the wilderness. And He was in the wilderness forty**
days, being tempted by Satan; and He was with the
wild animals, and the angels ministered to Him.

Immediately after His baptism, the Lord Jesus was thrust
into the wilderness by the Holy Spirit (Mark 1:12-13). From
that time onward, He fulfilled His ministry by living, moving,
and working in the Holy Spirit.

As the One living and moving by the Holy Spirit, the Lord
Jesus preached the gospel (1:14-20). In His preaching He sowed
the incarnated God as the seed for the kingdom of God. He
sowed into men's hearts a seed that would grow and develop
into the kingdom of God.

In the Holy Spirit the Lord Jesus taught the truth (1:21-22).
For Him to teach the truth was to enlighten darkened mankind and to disperse man's darkness.

The Lord Jesus also cast out demons (1:23-28). This casting out of demons was for the purpose of spreading the kingdom of God.

In His ministry the Lord Jesus healed the sick (1:29-39). To
heal the sick is to enliven the dead, to make the dead alive.

According to the Gospel of Mark, the Lord cleansed the
leper (1:40-45). To cleanse the leper is to sanctify the enlivened one. The Lord did this by forgiving sins, feasting with
sinners, being their joy in righteousness and life, satisfying
them, and liberating them. (*Life-study of Mark,* pp. 447-448)

Today's Reading

While the Lord Jesus was carrying out such a gospel ser-
vice, He was also binding Satan and plundering his kingdom.
Satan had no ground in Him. In Mark 3:22-30 we see that the
Lord bound Satan and plundered his house by the Holy Spirit.

In 3:31-35 we see that the Lord Jesus denied the natural
relationship. Instead of remaining in the relationship of the

natural life, He chose to be in the relationship of the spiritual life. This was the reason He could say, "Whoever does the will of God, this one is My brother and sister and mother" (3:35). The natural relationship was not given any ground in His living.

As the One who lived fully according to and for God's New Testament economy, the Lord Jesus suffered the world's rejection and hatred. In 6:1-6 He was despised by the Nazarenes. Elsewhere in this chapter we see that He suffered the world's rejection.

In 7:1-23 the Lord Jesus exposed man's inward condition, the evil condition of man's heart. He said, "That which goes out of the man, that defiles the man" (v. 20). Then He spoke concerning wicked things that proceed from within and defile a man (vv. 21-23).

After exposing the condition of man's heart, the Lord Jesus presented Himself as the life supply to a seeking one (7:24-30). In 7:27 He referred to Himself as the children's bread, that is, as our life supply. Hence, He presented Himself as the bread of life.

In 7:31-37 the Lord Jesus healed a deaf and dumb man, and in 8:22-26 He healed a blind man. In these instances the Lord healed specific organs of those who had been enlivened by Him.

In 8:27—9:13 the Lord Jesus is revealed as our universal and entire replacement. It is through His all-inclusive death and wonderful resurrection that we can take Him as such a replacement.

The Gospel of Mark presents the Lord Jesus as the One who accomplished an all-inclusive death. In His death He bore our sins, condemned sin, crucified the old man, terminated the old creation, destroyed Satan, judged the world, abolished the ordinances, and released the divine life. (*Life-study of Mark,* pp. 448-449)

Further Reading: Life-study of Mark, msg. 52

Enlightenment and inspiration: _____

_____

_____

_____

Morning Nourishment

Mark **So then the Lord Jesus, after speaking to them, was**
16:19-20 **taken up into heaven and sat at the right hand of**
God. And they went out and preached everywhere,
the Lord working with *them* and confirming the
word by the accompanying signs.

After the Lord accomplished this all-inclusive death, He entered into His wonderful resurrection. In and through His resurrection He regenerated His followers and germinated the new creation.

After His resurrection, the Lord Jesus "was taken up into heaven and sat at the right hand of God" (Mark 16:19). He now remains in His all-surpassing ascension to execute what He has accomplished through His death and resurrection.

The Lord Jesus did not enter into His death, resurrection, and ascension alone. Rather, He brought His followers into His death, and then He ushered them into His resurrection....His followers may now enjoy Him in His ascension as their life and life supply, the Lord of all, God's Christ, the Head of all to the church, the Head of the Body, the glorified One, the enthroned One, the One who is above all, and the One who fills all in all.

Through His death, resurrection, and ascension, and by bringing His followers into that death, resurrection, and ascension, the Lord Jesus has brought forth the new man as the reality of the kingdom of God. First, this new man issues in the church. Then, in the coming age, the new man will develop into the millennium. Ultimately, in the new heaven and the new earth, the new man will consummate in the New Jerusalem. This will be our eternal destiny, and this is also the conclusion of the Scriptures. (*Life-study of Mark*, pp. 449, 452)

Today's Reading

The Gospel of Mark...conveys a heavenly vision...that should direct our steps, control our living, and bring us into God's consummation. This vision is able to keep us in God's economy so that we may live the church life with the goal of reaching the millennium and the New Jerusalem.

Such a vision from God will always direct our steps and control our living. This was true even in the Old Testament, where we are told that without vision the people will perish (Prov. 29:18a, KJV). Under the heavenly vision we are directed toward God's destination, and our life is controlled according to God's economy.

The vision of God's economy...has become the principle that directs our steps and that governs our way....Because we have seen this vision, throughout the years heavenly light has been flooding into the Lord's recovery....[This is because] we are under this vision. Whenever we come to the Word of God, the light shines because we are in this directing, controlling, governing vision.

The Gospel of Mark reveals a life that is fully according to and for God's New Testament economy. This life is not merely righteous, holy, spiritual, and victorious....The Gospel of Mark presents the person of the God-man, the One who lived, acted, moved, and worked step by step according to God's economy.

The Gospel of Mark records how the Lord was examined by different parties. But no one could find fault with Him. As we consider the Gospel of Mark, we also are not able to find any fault, defect, or deficiency in the Lord's living related to God's economy....[Many] tried to find fault with the Lord Jesus according to Jewish law and practice and according to Roman politics. Let us examine Him according to the measure of the New Testament economy, of a standard that is much more strict. If we were to examine the Lord in this way, we would not find any shortcoming with Him. He not only fulfilled the law—He fulfilled God's economy.

This vision should become the yardstick, the standard, by which we measure matters related to the Christian life. If we have this vision, we shall see that it is not sufficient simply to be righteous, holy, spiritual, and victorious....May we all see the vision of God's New Testament economy and see in the Gospel of Mark a portrait of a life fully according to and for God's economy. (*Life-study of Mark*, pp. 452-454)

Further Reading: Life-study of Mark, msg. 52

Enlightenment and inspiration: _____

_____

_____

_____

Morning Nourishment

1 Cor. **But of Him you are in Christ Jesus, who became**
1:30 **wisdom to us from God: both righteousness and**
sanctification and redemption.

Gal. **I am crucified with Christ; and** *it is* **no longer I** *who*
2:20 **live, but** *it is* **Christ** *who* **lives in me; and the** *life* **which**
I now live in the flesh I live in faith, the *faith* **of the Son**
of God, who loved me and gave Himself up for me.

After Christ's ascension, His disciples continued His life, a life
of preaching, teaching, casting out demons, healing the sick, and
cleansing the lepers. This is the significance of Mark 16:20: "And
they went out and preached everywhere, the Lord working with
them and confirming the word by the accompanying signs." Here
we have the continuation of the life of the Lord Jesus recorded in
the Gospel of Mark. This life, a life according to and for God's New
Testament economy, has not ceased, for it is continued by those
who believe in the Lord.

In the past nineteen centuries, many matters have come in to
frustrate, damage, and even replace in the lives of Christians the
unique life that is according to God's New Testament economy.
These hindering matters include culture, religion, ethics, morality, philosophy, the improvement of character, and the effort to be
spiritual, scriptural, holy, and victorious.

We need to have a clear view of the kind of life we should be
living....All of us have been distracted from God's economy by
certain of these things. (*Life-study of Mark*, pp. 521-522)

Today's Reading

All Christians have been frustrated and damaged by the good
that is related to the tree of the knowledge of good and evil. The
tree that is versus the tree of life is not merely the tree of the
knowledge of evil; it is the tree of the knowledge of both good and
evil. In fact, the word "good" is mentioned before evil in Genesis
2:17. This indicates that good things as well as evil things can
keep us from enjoying the tree of life. In our experience as Christians, good things may actually hinder us much more than evil

things. Those who love the Lord may not touch what is evil, but day by day they may allow something good to replace the tree of life in their experience. Are not culture, religion, ethics, morality, philosophy, and the improvement of character good things? Certainly they are. To be sure, trying to be spiritual, scriptural, holy, and victorious is good. Nevertheless, anything apart from the life-giving Spirit is a frustration to the life that is fully according to and for God's New Testament economy.

God has put us into Christ not that we may live a life of good things, but that we may live a life that is uniquely, wholly, and absolutely of Christ. God has put us into Christ so that we may live a life of Christ to carry out His New Testament economy.

Although more than nineteen centuries have passed since Christ's ascension, He still has not come back. God's people are not yet ready for the Lord's coming. For centuries those who love the Lord Jesus have been hindered by different kinds of good things. These good things have occupied those who love the Lord and seek Him. Christians who love God and seek the Lord do not care for worldly things....[However], some Christians are preoccupied with ethics, morality, and improvement of character; others are distracted from the Lord by their efforts to be spiritual, scriptural, holy, and victorious. How few really care for the living person of Christ Himself!

Mark presents a portrait of a life that is fully according to and for God's New Testament economy. In eternity past God the Father put us into the One who lived such a life. Now we should be the continuation of this life....The life we live should not be a life of culture, religion, ethics, morality, philosophy, or improvement of character...[or] even...a life of trying to be spiritual, scriptural, holy, and victorious. The life we live today should be Christ Himself. Only a life that is Christ is fully according to the New Testament economy of God. Any other kind of life, no matter how good it may be, is short of God's economy. (*Life-study of Mark*, pp. 522-523)

Further Reading: Life-study of Mark, msg. 61

Enlightenment and inspiration: _____

_____

_____

_____

Morning Nourishment

Rom. For the mind set on the flesh is death, but the mind
8:6 set on the spirit is life and peace.

Col. When Christ our life is manifested, then you also will
3:4   be manifested with Him in glory.

Phil. For to me, to live is Christ and to die is gain.
1:21

In the Gospel of Mark we see a life that is the substance of God's New Testament economy....The life the Lord Jesus lived was the expression of God. According to the Gospel of Mark, there is no indication that the Lord Jesus was living merely in a way to keep the law, that He did certain things simply because they were required by the law. Furthermore, [it] does not indicate that the Lord Jesus only lived a good life....The Lord Jesus lived God, and He expressed God. Whatever He did was God's doing from within Him and through Him. This means that all that the Lord Jesus did was not merely the keeping of the law or the doing of good in an ethical sense. The Lord Jesus was a person who lived God and expressed Him in all that He said and did.

There has never been another life like that of the Lord Jesus. The biographies of other people may indicate that they were good or that they tried to keep the law of God. But the Lord Jesus is the only One who lived God and expressed Him in a full way. Of course, the Lord never broke the law, and He never did anything wrong. Nevertheless, the crucial matter regarding His life was not that He kept the law or that He did good. The crucial point is that He lived God and expressed Him. The Lord's living was not in the kingdom of law-keeping or of doing good. He lived altogether in another kingdom, the kingdom of God. (*Life-study of Mark,* pp. 463-464)

Today's Reading

Those who live in the kingdom of God have God as their life, and they live Him. God lives in them, through them, and out of them. As a result, they live a life that expresses nothing other than God Himself. God is the real holiness, morality, and ethics. Therefore, to have God as life and to live Him is to live in a way that is higher than human morality or ethics.

Only the kind of life that lives God and expresses Him produces the Body of Christ. Any other way of living always damages the Body. Throughout its history the church has been divided not mainly by evil things, but primarily by good things that are not God Himself. If all Christians would care only for God Himself and for having Him as life and living Him, there would not be any divisions among believers.

The reason there would be no divisions if we all cared only for God Himself is that God is one. In Ephesians 4:4-6 Paul speaks of the one Body, the one Spirit, the one Lord, and the one God and Father. If we see the oneness in Ephesians 4, we shall know how to keep the oneness of the Body of Christ, a oneness that is actually the Triune God Himself. If we all have God as our holiness, righteousness, and everything to us, there will not be any divisions among us. However, if we have something other than God, there will be divisions. Anything that we have other than God Himself is a factor of division.

It is God's intention in His recovery to bring us back to His New Testament economy. The pattern for God's New Testament economy is found in the life of the Lord Jesus....In the entire New Testament there is only one person who lived fully, wholly, and absolutely according to the New Testament economy of God, and this person was the Lord Jesus.

The Lord Jesus...lived God the Father as His life. This kind of living is much superior to a life of living the law or human morality....He had God the Father within Him and God the Spirit upon Him. His life...was fully according to God's New Testament economy. Hallelujah for such a life! This life is the reality, substance, and pattern of God's New Testament economy. It is the life that produces the members of Christ to form His Body to express the Triune God. (*Life-study of Mark*, pp. 464-465, 467-468)

Further Reading: Life-study of Mark, msgs. 53-54

Enlightenment and inspiration: _____

_____

_____

_____

Hymns, #501

1　O glorious Christ, Savior mine,
　　Thou art truly radiance divine;
　　God infinite, in eternity,
　　Yet man in time, finite to be.

　　　　Oh! Christ, expression of God, the Great,
　　　　Inexhaustible, rich, and sweet!
　　　　God mingled with humanity
　　　　Lives in me my all to be.

2　The fulness of God dwells in Thee;
　　Thou dost manifest God's glory;
　　In flesh Thou hast redemption wrought;
　　As Spirit, oneness with me sought.

3　All things of the Father are Thine;
　　All Thou art in Spirit is mine;
　　The Spirit makes Thee real to me,
　　That Thou experienced might be.

4　The Spirit of life causes Thee
　　By Thy Word to transfer to me.
　　Thy Spirit touched, Thy word received,
　　Thy life in me is thus conceived.

5　In spirit while gazing on Thee,
　　As a glass reflecting Thy glory,
　　Like to Thyself transformed I'll be,
　　That Thou might be expressed thru me.

6　In no other way could we be
　　Sanctified and share Thy vict'ry;
　　Thus only spiritual we'll be
　　And touch the life of glory.

7　Thy Spirit will me saturate,
　　Every part will God permeate,
　　Deliv'ring me from the old man,
　　With all saints building for His plan.

Composition for prophecy with main point and sub-points: _____

A Life Fully according to and for
God's New Testament Economy (2)

Scripture Reading: Mark 4:1-20, 26-29; 12:30

Day 1 I. **God's New Testament economy is to sow the living person of Christ into our being so that we may live a life that is fully according to and for God's New Testament economy (Mark 4:1-20, 26-29):**

A. Christ as the Sower is the Messenger of God, Christ as the seed is the message of God as the gospel of God, and Christ sown into our being to grow and develop in us is the building of God and the kingdom of God as the goal of God (Luke 17:20-24; Mal. 1:1; 3:1-3; Heb. 1:2; 1 Cor. 3:6-9; 2 Sam. 7:12-14a).

B. Christ as the Sower has sown Himself as the life-giving Spirit into us; the life-giving Spirit in our spirit is the seed of a life that lives fully according to and for God's New Testament economy (John 14:6a; 10:10b; 1 Cor. 15:45b; 1 John 3:9; 5:11-12; 1 Pet. 1:23; Gal. 2:20; Phil. 1:21a; Rom. 8:2, 4, 6).

C. The Lord's recovery is not a work, teaching, theology, or movement; the Lord's recovery is the living Christ as the seed of life sown into our being.

D. The kingdom of God, which is Christ Himself as the life-giving Spirit, is a seed; the kingdom comes by the growth of the indwelling Christ in us (Mark 4:26; Luke 17:20-24; 1 Cor. 15:45b).

E. We must give the Lord our full cooperation for the inward operation of His growth process in us so that we may hasten His coming (Gal. 1:15-16a; 2:20; 4:19; Rev. 19:7; 2 Pet. 3:11-12; cf. Luke 12:32).

Day 2 II. **In order to live a life that is fully according to and for God's New Testament economy,**

we must allow the indwelling Christ as the
seed of life to grow in the soil of our entire
heart, thus making our heart His home and a
duplication of God's heart (Mark 4:1-20;
12:30; Eph. 3:16-17):

A. Although man's heart is corrupt and deceitful
   and its condition is incurable (Jer. 17:9; Mark
   7:21-23), even such a heart can be a tablet upon
   which God writes His law of life (Jer. 31:33;
   cf. 2 Cor. 3:3) by the spontaneous growth of Christ
   as the seed of life in man's heart (Mark 4:26-29);
   this is God's way, according to His economy, to
   deal with the heart of fallen man.

B. We must deal with the condition of our heart to
   make our heart the good earth for the full
   growth of Christ in us (Col. 2:19; Gal. 4:19):

   1. The wayside signifies the heart that is
      hardened by worldly traffic and cannot open
      to understand, to comprehend, the word of
      the kingdom; the birds signify the evil one,
      Satan, who comes and snatches away the
      word of the kingdom sown in the hardened
      heart (Mark 4:3-4, 15):

      a. The anti-God world system with its
         worldly traffic is the system of Satan,
         who is the ruler of the world; we must
         be strengthened into our spirit, our
         inner man, and remain in our spirit
         so that we can overcome the world and
         be kept from the evil one by remaining
         in the pneumatic Christ for Him to
         make His home in our heart (1 John
         2:14-15; 5:4, 18; John 12:31; 14:30; Eph.
         3:16-17a).

      b. We need to let the word of Christ dwell in
         us richly; His word works in us to sepa-
         rate us from anything worldly and to sat-
         urate us with the reality of the Triune
         God (Col. 3:16; John 17:17; Eph. 5:26).

Day 3

2. The rocky places that do not have much earth signify the heart that is shallow in receiving the Lord's word, having "no root" (Mark 4:5-6, 16-17):

   a. The sun with its scorching heat signifies affliction or persecution; the scorching heat of the sun causes the seed that is not rooted to wither.

   b. The heat of the sun is for the growth and ripening of the crop, which take place once the seed has been deeply rooted, but because of the seed's lack of root, the sun's heat, which should cause growth and ripening, becomes a deathblow to the seed.

   c. In order to have Christ as the seed of life deeply rooted in us, we need to be deeply rooted in Him by having a secret life and secret history with Him (Col. 2:7; S. S. 4:12; Psa. 31:20; 32:7; 83:3; 91:1; 119:114).

   d. We must take time in secret to absorb Him, setting aside time every morning to have direct and intimate fellowship with the Lord in pray-reading His word and interceding for the interests of God's economy (Mark 1:35; Matt. 6:6; Psa. 5:3; 27:4; 46:5; 59:16; 88:13; 90:14; 119:148; 143:8; 1 Kings 8:48).

Day 4

3. The thorns signify the anxieties of the age, the deceitfulness of riches, and the lusts for other things, which utterly choke the word, preventing it from growing in the heart and causing it to become unfruitful (Mark 4:7, 18-19):

   a. Anxiety is the gear that makes the world move; to allow the Lord to deal with our anxiety is to allow Him to deal with the gear of our human life; our human life is a life of anxiety, whereas God's life is a life of enjoyment, rest, comfort, and satisfaction; we must habitually fellowship with God in prayer to be infused with Him as life and peace, the antidote to anxiety (Phil. 4:6-7; John 16:33).

b. To be deceived by riches is to suppose "godliness to be a means of gain"; because of pride and the desire for profit, for riches, some today are teaching differently; to maintain the victorious standard of the church, we need to be lovers of God for the economy of God, not lovers of money for the system of Satan (1 Tim. 6:3-10; 2 Tim. 3:1-5).

Day 5
&
Day 6

4. The good earth signifies a heart that gives every inch of its ground to receive the word that the word may grow, bear fruit, and produce even a hundredfold (Mark 4:8-9, 20, 26-29; Luke 8:15):

a. Today in the Lord's recovery the Lord is sowing Himself into people so that He may have the good earth to grow Himself into the kingdom.

b. Day by day and morning and evening, we must keep our heart open to the Lord by repenting and confessing all our sins to Him; this is the way to deal with our heart to make it the good earth for the growth of Christ as the seed of life (Mark 1:4-5, 15; 2 Cor. 3:16; 1 John 1:9).

c. Giving the Lord the full way to grow in our heart will make our heart the duplicate of God's heart, and we will live a life fully according to and for God's New Testament economy to carry out His heart's desire (*Hymns,* #395, #1132).

Morning Nourishment

Mark 4:3 Listen! Behold, the sower went out to sow.
14 The sower sows the word.
26 And He said, So is the kingdom of God: as if a man cast seed on the earth.

Matthew 13 reveals that Christ has sown Himself as the seed into us as the soil. Christ is the seed, and we are the soil with the nutrients for the growth of the seed. Christ in resurrection, Christ as the life-giving Spirit, has sown Himself into us not simply to stay in us but to grow in us. The growth of Christ in us equals the building.

The Christ who has sown Himself into us is now doing a particular work in us—the work of making His home in our inner being, in our hearts (Eph. 3:17). This is building, and it is carried out through the mingling of divinity with humanity. Such a building is mentioned in John 14:23: "If anyone loves Me,...My Father will love him, and We will come to him and make an abode with him." This abode is not only for the Triune God but is also for us. Hence, it is a mutual abode. (*Life-study of 1 & 2 Samuel,* pp. 191-192)

Today's Reading

The Lord's recovery is not work, teaching, or theology. It is a seed; it is the living Christ as a seed. I have the assurance to declare to the whole universe that the all-inclusive Christ as the life-giving Spirit has been sown...in America, Europe, Brazil, and many other places. No one and nothing can stop it. The Lord's recovery is not a movement. It is Christ Himself as the seed of life sown into our being. The sower is Christ, and the seed is also Christ, Christ in the word sown into us to make us the sons of the kingdom. (*Life-study of Matthew,* p. 441)

In Mark 1:1 and 14 we read of the gospel of Jesus Christ and the gospel of God. This gospel is also the gospel of the kingdom of God. Not many Christians have realized that the kingdom of God is a person. The kingdom eventually becomes a corporate person. The seed of the kingdom is an individual, the Lord Jesus. As the Sower, He came to sow Himself as the seed of the kingdom into His disciples. Now this seed is developing into the corporate kingdom of God. This kingdom is actually the Body of Christ. The development of the Lord as the seed of the kingdom is His Body, and His Body is His increase, His enlargement.

This understanding of the kingdom of God is certainly different from the traditional concept of the kingdom. According to the New Testament, the kingdom of God is the enlargement of the person of Christ. The kingdom is the development of the seed, which is Jesus Christ. Today this development of Christ is the church. Hence, the church as Christ's Body is the kingdom of God.

As the One who is the seed of the kingdom of God, the Lord Jesus lived a life that is altogether different from a life of culture, religion, ethics, morality, improvement of character, philosophy, and the effort to be spiritual, scriptural, holy, and victorious. The life He lived was according to God's New Testament economy.... God's economy is a matter of the dispensing of Himself—the Triune God—into His believers.

Only the kind of life lived by the Lord Jesus is a life in which the Triune God is dispensed into God's chosen people. A living that is according to culture, religion, ethics, and morality is not the living that dispenses God into man....Confucius, for example, taught ethics, and he behaved in a moral, ethical way. Nevertheless, in his living there was not the dispensing of the Triune God into people. The same is true with respect to those who lived a life of philosophy or improvement of character, and even of those who tried to be spiritual, scriptural, holy, and victorious. Praise the Lord that in His life there was the dispensing of the Triune God into His chosen people!

The gospel, which is a new beginning, terminates all the old things. When the Lord Jesus was baptized, the old things were buried. In His living after His baptism, a living that was according to the New Testament economy of God, the Lord Jesus sowed Himself as the seed of life into His believers. (*Life-study of Mark*, pp. 528-530)

Further Reading: Life-study of Mark, msgs. 62, 57-58; *Life-study of 1 & 2 Samuel,* msgs. 29-30*

Enlightenment and inspiration: _____

_____

_____

_____

Morning Nourishment

Mark And as he sowed, some *seed* fell beside the way, and
4:4 the birds came and devoured it.
  15 ...These are...beside the way, where the word is sown;
      and when they hear, immediately Satan comes and
      takes away the word which has been sown into them.

Beside the way is the place close to the way. Because it is hardened by the traffic of the way, it is difficult for the seeds to penetrate
it. This kind of wayside signifies the heart that is hardened by the
worldly traffic and does not open to understand, to comprehend,
the word of the kingdom (Matt. 13:19). The birds signify the evil
one, Satan, who came and snatched away the word of the kingdom
sown in the hardened heart. (*Life-study of Matthew*, p. 442)

Today's Reading

Because the wayside, part of the soil for farming, was so close
to the traffic, it became hardened by the traffic. This made it
impossible for the seed to penetrate it. Thus, the seed remained
on the surface of the wayside. This signifies those who are not
poor in spirit or pure in heart because they have so much worldly
traffic. Education, commerce, politics, science, business, and other
kinds of worldly traffic go back and forth within their mind, emotion, and will. They are occupied with promotion, position, and
ambition. For this reason, it is very difficult to preach the gospel to
those in politics. The politicians have too much worldly traffic in
their being....Likewise, it is difficult to preach the gospel to those
on Wall Street. Unless the Lord knocks them down, they are too
hard to receive the word into them. Day and night they are preoccupied with figures, money, and business. They cannot be poor in
spirit or pure in heart....When you attempt to sow the seed into
them, the seed cannot penetrate them. There is no room in them
for the seed. This is also true among so many in education, especially those pursuing a doctoral degree. There has been so much
traffic in their heart that their heart has been hardened, just like
the wayside in the Lord's parable. Although they may hear the
gospel of Christ, not a word can penetrate their heart.

We thank the Lord that, in His mercy, when the gospel was preached to us, we were poor in spirit and pure in heart. On the day I was saved by the Lord, I said to Him, "If the whole world could be mine, I would not take it. I don't want it and I don't like it. Lord, I want to keep my heart for You. I don't like to have any worldly traffic in my heart." It is never good to have traffic through farmland. No farmer would allow this. Are you part of the wayside? Do not stay close to the way. Stay in the center of the farm. Then the worldly traffic will not touch you. (*Life-study of Matthew,* pp. 442-443)

In the parable of the sower the people who receive the Lord Jesus are likened to four kinds of earth. The first is the wayside, the margin of the field. This margin or border of the field lies between the field and the road and is somewhat neutral, being neither the road nor the field. Because this kind of earth is close to the road, it has been trodden down by the traffic of the world and has become hardened and preoccupied, making it difficult for the seed to get in. The birds of the air realize this situation and come immediately to snatch away the seed. When some people listen to the word of the gospel of the kingdom, their hearts are preoccupied by the worldly communication and traffic. They may listen to the message and nod their heads in agreement, but their hearts have been hardened. After the message is over, they retain nothing because the word has been snatched out of their heart. The Lord Jesus told us definitely that the birds in the air signify the evil one, Satan (Matt. 13:4, 19). Satan moves upon the earth, but he dwells in the air. From there he watches over the earth. Satan never sleeps; he is always working on the earth, watching for an opportunity to snatch the word of the kingdom from the hardened hearts. The worldly traffic with all of its complications hardens the hearts of men. We need to pray: "Lord Jesus, keep me from being the wayside. Don't let my heart be hardened by the traffic of this world." (*The Kingdom,* pp. 105-106)

Further Reading: Life-study of Matthew, msg. 36; *The Kingdom,* ch. 11

Enlightenment and inspiration: _____

_____

_____

_____

Morning Nourishment

Mark And other *seed* fell on the rocky place, where it did
4:5-6 not have much earth, and immediately it sprang
up because it had no depth of earth. And when the
sun rose, it was scorched; and because it had no
root, it withered.

16-17 And likewise, these are the ones being sown on the
rocky places, who, when they hear the word,
immediately receive it with joy. Yet they have no
root in themselves, but last only for a time; then
when affliction or persecution occurs because of
the word, immediately they are stumbled.

The rocky places that do not have much earth signify the heart
that is shallow in receiving the word of the kingdom, because deep
within are rocks—hidden sins, personal desires, self-seeking, and
self-pity—which frustrate the seed from gaining root in the depth
of the heart. The sun with its scorching heat signifies affliction or
persecution (Matt. 13:21), which dries up the seed that is not
rooted. The heat of the sun is for the growth and ripening of the
crop once the seed is deeply rooted. But due to the seed's lack of
root, the sun's growing and ripening heat becomes a death blow to
the seed. (*Life-study of Matthew,* pp. 443-444)

Today's Reading

The second type of earth corresponds to the temper, lust, self,
and flesh—the things hidden in our heart. Perhaps not many
among us are part of the wayside, but I am very concerned that a
good number may be rocky places. In appearance they are the
same as others, for the soil is on the surface. But they have no
depth. Rather, they have lust, temper, self, and flesh. All these are
rocks hidden beneath the soil. Therefore, the first type of soil corresponds to those who are not poor in spirit and pure in heart, and
the second corresponds to those who still have their temper, lust,
sin, self, and flesh beneath the surface. Some of you may still be
hiding your lust, your selfishness, and your flesh. You may shout
hallelujahs in the meetings, but you do not have much depth.

Instead of depth, there are rocks. Sooner or later, all these rocks will be exposed because the word that has been sown into you will not be able to be rooted in you. You may be happy and joyful, shouting praises to the Lord, but there is no root in you. Hence, when the affliction and persecutions come, you will be dried up like a plant without root that withers under the scorching heat of the sun. May the Lord have mercy upon us and dig out all the hidden rocks. May He dig out our temper, lust, self, flesh, and any other negative thing so that there may be room in our heart for the seed to be rooted deeply within us. (*Life-study of Matthew*, p. 444)

The second reason for barrenness is the lack of roots. What is a root? In a tree, the part that can be seen is the trunk, while the part beneath the ground, which cannot be seen, is the root. The branches have life and are visible; the roots are invisible. The roots are buried in the earth. Therefore, the roots refer to the *hidden life*. Those who do not have any root before the Lord will be dried up in their life. Those who do not have a hidden life, who do everything before men and have nothing special before the Lord, cannot stand the test of the cross. Brothers and sisters, let me ask you honestly, is your living only what is seen by men? Do you have any secret life before the Lord, inside your own room? If your prayers can only be heard in the prayer meetings, if you only read your Bible to others, and if your works are all before men, you do not have any roots....Nothing can preserve you as much as a hidden life. If you see that a brother has fallen or failed, or has come into trouble, without asking anyone, you can surely say that prior to this trouble he lost his hidden life....Your spiritual life depends very much on your hidden life before God. If you cannot sustain a hidden life, you will be weak before the Lord. Therefore, you should realize the importance of the hidden life. (*The Collected Works of Watchman Nee*, vol. 11, pp. 834-835)

Further Reading: The Collected Works of Watchman Nee, vol. 11, pp. 823-841; vol. 38, ch. 66; *The Kingdom,* ch. 11

Enlightenment and inspiration: _____

_____

_____

_____

Morning Nourishment

Mark   And other *seed* fell into the thorns, and the thorns
4:7   came up and utterly choked it, and it yielded no fruit.
18-19   And others are the ones being sown into the thorns;
         these are the ones who have heard the word, and the
         anxieties of the age and the deceitfulness of riches
         and the lusts for other things enter in and utterly
         choke the word, and it becomes unfruitful.
1 Tim.   But godliness with contentment is great gain.
6:6

   The thorns here signify the anxiety of the age and the deceitfulness of riches, which choke the word from growing in the heart and
cause it to become unfruitful....Several times in...[Matthew 6:19-
34], the words "anxious" or "anxiety" are used. The Lord tells us not
to be anxious about our living, about what we shall eat, drink, or
wear. The third type of soil is not as bad as the second, but it is still
difficult for the seed to grow in it because of anxiety and the
deceitfulness of riches. All these thorns must be uprooted. If the
anxiety of this age and the deceitfulness of riches are rooted out of
our heart, the seed will grow. (*Life-study of Matthew*, pp. 444-445)

Today's Reading

   The parable of the sower seems very simple, but it is actually
deep and profound. It exposes the real condition of our heart in
the presence of the heavenly King. Whatever is in us is exposed.
This parable covers the hardness by the worldly traffic; the
hidden lust, self, and flesh; and the anxiety of the age and deceitfulness of money. These are the wayside, the rocks, and the
thorns. As long as you are either the wayside, the soil with hidden
rocks, or the soil with thorns, the kingdom cannot grow in you. In
other words, the church cannot grow in those types of soil. In
order for the church to grow, the seed must fall on good earth.

   There is no anxiety in the divine life and the divine nature.
Anxiety is not of the divine life, but of the human life, just as bark-
ing is of the dog life, not of the bird life. Our human life is a life of
anxiety, whereas God's life is a life of enjoyment, rest, comfort, and
satisfaction....With [God], there is no such thing as anxiety....

Although God has many desires, He has no anxiety. Our human life, on the contrary, is virtually composed of anxiety; it is constituted with it. Take anxiety away from a human being and the result will be death. A dead man has no anxiety. A figure in a wax museum or a statue in front of a Catholic cathedral has no anxiety, but as long as you are a living person, you cannot escape from anxiety.

In His speaking in chapter six of Matthew, the Lord apparently is dealing with the matter of riches. In reality, however, He is touching the matter of anxiety, the basic problem of our human living....Matthew 6:19-34 seemingly touches our wealth, our riches; actually, the Lord's intention here is to touch anxiety, the source of the problem of our daily living. The whole world is involved with anxiety. Anxiety is the gear that makes the world move. It is the incentive for all human culture. If there were no anxiety regarding our living, no one would do anything. Rather, everyone would be idle. Thus, by touching our anxiety, the Lord touches the gear of human life. (*Life-study of Matthew*, pp. 445, 274-275)

In [1 Timothy 6:]5 Paul refers to those who suppose "godliness to be a means of gain." They make godliness a way of gain—material profit, a gain-making trade. The desire for material gain is another reason certain ones teach differently. Thus, because of pride and the desire for profit, for riches, some today are teaching differently. Pride is related to wanting a name and a good reputation, and gain is related to money and material profit.

In verse 6 Paul says, "But godliness with contentment is great gain." Concerning the expression "contentment," Vincent says, "An inward self-sufficiency, as opposed to the lack or the desire of outward things. It was a favourite Stoic word." The expression "great gain" means great means of gain. It mainly denotes the blessings in this age—godliness plus self-sufficiency and the ability to be free from greediness and the cares of this age. (*Life-study of 1 Timothy*, p. 96)

Further Reading: Life-study of Matthew, msg. 22; *The Kingdom,* ch. 12; *Life-study of 1 Timothy,* msg. 11

Enlightenment and inspiration: _____
_____
_____

Morning Nourishment

Mark   And others fell into the good earth and yielded
4:8   fruit, coming up and growing; and one bore
       thirtyfold, and one sixtyfold, and one a hundred-
       fold.
20   And these are the ones sown on the good earth:
       those who hear the word and receive *it* and bear
       fruit, one thirtyfold, and one sixtyfold, and one
       a hundredfold.

The good earth signifies the good heart that is not hardened by worldly traffic, that is without hidden sins, and that
is without the anxiety of the age and the deceitfulness of
riches. Such a heart gives every inch of its ground to receive
the word that the word may grow, bear fruit, and produce
even a hundredfold (Matt. 13:23). The good heart is a heart
which has no worldly traffic, no rocks, and no thorns. It has
no hidden sins, selfishness, lust, or flesh and no anxiety of
the age or deceitfulness of money. This kind of heart is truly
pure to match the spirit. Such a heart is the good soil that
grows Christ. Christ as the seed of life can grow only in this
kind of heart, this kind of soil. This is the soil that can grow
the kingdom. (*Life-study of Matthew,* pp. 445-446)

Today's Reading

In the United States of America there are millions of
Christians. Recently a magazine said that there are fifty mil-
lion regenerated Christians in this country. Only the Lord
knows how many among this number are genuine Christians. Although there are so many Christians, I wonder how
many are the good earth. How many have no worldly traffic,
no hidden sins, flesh, lusts, or self, and no anxiety or deceitfulness of money? How many are poor in spirit and pure in
heart? It is very difficult to find such Christians. Although

we may be surrounded with Christians, we rarely find one who is truly poor in spirit and pure in heart. How about you? Do you still have worldly traffic in your heart? Are you truly poor in spirit and pure in heart? Are there any hidden rocks deep within? What about the anxiety of this age and the deceitfulness of money? Although we must consider these questions, we should not be discouraged. Rather, we should be encouraged. Nothing can stop God's economy. There will be at least some who are the good earth. According to the percentage indicated by the Lord's parable, this is twenty-five percent of the believers. I would be happy with even five percent. How good it would be if among all the real Christians five percent were poor in spirit and pure in heart, had no hidden self, flesh, or sin, and had no anxiety or deceitfulness of money! How wonderful it would be if five percent were pure for Christ to grow in them! Here and there, in so many major cities, the Lord will find the good earth. The Lord is merciful. We might have had too much traffic, but the Lord saved us from the wayside and placed us in the center of the farmland. I know of many brothers and sisters in whom the Lord has dug out all the hidden things and uprooted all the thorns to make their heart the good earth. Praise the Lord for this! There is no doubt that among us a good many are the good earth, the good soil. The kingdom and the church are growing here. Here in the church life we are growing Christ, and we are growing the kingdom. The kingdom does not come by our working. It comes only by the growth of Christ within us. May we all be impressed that today in the Lord's recovery the Lord is doing the work of sowing Himself into people so that He may have the good earth to grow Himself into the kingdom. This is the first parable, and this is the preliminary work for the establishment of the kingdom of the heavens. (*Life-study of Matthew*, pp. 446-447)

Further Reading: Life-study of Matthew, msg. 36

Enlightenment and inspiration: _____

_____

_____

_____

Morning Nourishment

Mark ...**The kingdom of God has drawn near. Repent**
1:15 **and believe in the gospel.**

The Lord's intention is to sow Himself as the seed of life into
us. We are the living earth, the living soil, the living ground. The
spirit is enclosed by the heart, so if the Lord is going to come into
us, our heart has to be opened. We can open our heart to the Lord
by repenting and confessing. The word repent in the Greek lan-
guage means to have a change of mind or a turn of mind. Our
mind was originally not toward the Lord but toward something
else, and our mind was fixed. Now we have to repent, which
means we have to have a change of mind, and we have to turn our
mind. This means the mind is open to the Lord. Following our
repentance, we will always confess. We need to confess all our failures, sins, and shortcomings to the Lord. Confession is the exercise of the conscience. When we repent by turning our mind, we
will immediately confess by exercising our conscience. Then there
is an opening of the heart. When we mean business to repent to
the Lord and confess all our failures before God, our emotion will
immediately be moved and touched. We will tell the Lord, "Lord
Jesus, I love You." When our emotion is moved, our will makes a
decision for the Lord. We will say, "Lord, from today I want
nothing besides You. I want You to be my aim, my goal, and my
one desire. I only want to seek after You." The mind of the heart
turns, the conscience of the heart is opened, and the emotion and
will of the heart follow. Thus, the whole heart is open to the Lord,
and the Lord has a way to come into our heart. It is by repenting
and confessing that we open our heart to the Lord. This is
revealed in the Scriptures and proven by our experience. (*The
Tree of Life,* p. 124)

Today's Reading

The sad thing is that with many of us, soon after the Lord
came into us, we became closed to Him....Gradually our emotion,...our will,...our mind,...and our conscience became closed to
Him. Thus, the Lord was imprisoned in our spirit. This is why

both in the Old and New Testaments the Lord always calls us to repent....Day by day and morning and evening we have to repent. To repent means to turn our mind to the Lord, to open our mind. Following this our conscience will be exercised in a thorough confession of our sins. Then our emotion will follow to love the Lord and our will will follow to choose the Lord. The result will be that our heart will be fully opened to the Lord, and the Lord will have a way to fill us with Himself. This is the way to deal with our heart to make it the good ground for the Lord as the seed of life to grow in. (*The Tree of Life*, pp. 124-125)

When someone attains a high position, there is always a question as to whether he will allow someone else to come in to match him or to be above him. If you had been Samuel, would you have given any ground for someone to match you or be above you? Samuel was pure and single. He was a Nazarite according to his mother's vow and was altogether not self-seeking. He never sought to gain anything for himself. He had no heart for anything besides God and God's elect. God loved Israel, and His heart was duplicated in Samuel.

Because God's heart was duplicated in Samuel, Samuel did not care for his own interest or gain. At the end, Samuel gained nothing but a tomb to be buried in. Due to the situation at the time, Samuel appointed his sons to be judges, but, contrary to Saul, he had no intention to build up a kingdom for them. His sons did not follow in his ways but went after unjust gain, took bribes, and perverted justice (1 Sam. 8:1-3). When the people asked Samuel to appoint a king, he was not offended by anything related to his sons; on the contrary, he was offended by their desire to replace God (vv. 4-7). Because he had no intention to build up a kingdom for his descendants, Samuel's concern was not for his children but for God's people. In such a situation it was easy for God to bring in the kingdom. (*Life-study of 1 & 2 Samuel*, pp. 44-45)

Further Reading: The Tree of Life, ch. 13; *Life-study of 1 & 2 Samuel*, msg. 7

Enlightenment and inspiration: _____
_____
_____
_____

Hymns, #1132

1   Lord, teach us how to pray,
     Not as the nations do in vain,
     But turn us from our way,
     And cause us, Lord, to call on You each day—
       Lord Jesus, grow in us.

2   Lord, You're the seed of life;
     You've sown Yourself into our heart,
     And now You have a start;
     So day by day more life to us impart—
       Lord Jesus, grow in us.

3   Lord Jesus, soften us;
     You know the source from which we came.
     By calling on Your name,
     Lord, let no earth unturned nor rocks remain—
       Lord Jesus, grow in us.

4   Lord, how Your light makes clear
     That we could not but e'er fail You;
     Yet there's a message true,
     The seed of life within us will break through—
       Lord Jesus, grow in us.

5   Make us in spirit poor;
     Lord, take whate'er we think we know.
     We'll open to life's flow,
     And thus take in the life that makes us grow—
       Lord Jesus, grow in us.

6   Lord, make us pure in heart;
     For we'll be not content until
     You all our being fill,
     O Lord, renew our mind, emotion, will—
       Lord Jesus, grow in us.

7   Yes, Lord, impress our heart
     That we must take You in each day;
     The seed will have its way;
     Your growing brings the kingdom here to stay—
       Lord Jesus, grow in us.

8   Amen!—The growth in life!
     There's nothing that Your life can't do;
     Our every part renew.
     We'll make it, we'll make it just by You.
       Lord Jesus, grow in us.
       Lord Jesus, grow in us.

Composition for prophecy with main point and sub-points: _____

_____
_____
_____
_____
_____
_____
_____
_____
_____
_____
_____
_____
_____
_____
_____
_____
_____
_____
_____
_____
_____
_____
_____
_____
_____
_____
_____
_____
_____
_____
_____
_____

Reading Schedule for the Recovery Version of the Old Testament with Footnotes

Wk.	Lord's Day	Monday	Tuesday	Wednesday	Thursday	Friday	Saturday
1	☐ Gen 1:1-5	☐ 1:6-23	☐ 1:24-31	☐ 2:1-9	☐ 2:10-25	☐ 3:1-13	☐ 3:14-24
2	☐ 4:1-26	☐ 5:1-32	☐ 6:1-22	☐ 7:1—8:3	☐ 8:4-22	☐ 9:1-29	☐ 10:1-32
3	☐ 11:1-32	☐ 12:1-20	☐ 13:1-18	☐ 14:1-24	☐ 15:1-21	☐ 16:1-16	☐ 17:1-27
4	☐ 18:1-33	☐ 19:1-38	☐ 20:1-18	☐ 21:1-34	☐ 22:1-24	☐ 23:1—24:27	☐ 24:28-67
5	☐ 25:1-34	☐ 26:1-35	☐ 27:1-46	☐ 28:1-22	☐ 29:1-35	☐ 30:1-43	☐ 31:1-55
6	☐ 32:1-32	☐ 33:1—34:31	☐ 35:1-29	☐ 36:1-43	☐ 37:1-36	☐ 38:1—39:23	☐ 40:1—41:13
7	☐ 41:14-57	☐ 42:1-38	☐ 43:1-34	☐ 44:1-34	☐ 45:1-28	☐ 46:1-34	☐ 47:1-31
8	☐ 48:1-22	☐ 49:1-15	☐ 49:16-33	☐ 50:1-26	☐ Exo 1:1-22	☐ 2:1-25	☐ 3:1-22
9	☐ 4:1-31	☐ 5:1-23	☐ 6:1-30	☐ 7:1-25	☐ 8:1-32	☐ 9:1-35	☐ 10:1-29
10	☐ 11:1-10	☐ 12:1-14	☐ 12:15-36	☐ 12:37-51	☐ 13:1-22	☐ 14:1-31	☐ 15:1-27
11	☐ 16:1-36	☐ 17:1-16	☐ 18:1-27	☐ 19:1-25	☐ 20:1-26	☐ 21:1-36	☐ 22:1-31
12	☐ 23:1-33	☐ 24:1-18	☐ 25:1-22	☐ 25:23-40	☐ 26:1-14	☐ 26:15-37	☐ 27:1-21
13	☐ 28:1-21	☐ 28:22-43	☐ 29:1-21	☐ 29:22-46	☐ 30:1-10	☐ 30:11-38	☐ 31:1-17
14	☐ 31:18—32:35	☐ 33:1-23	☐ 34:1-35	☐ 35:1-35	☐ 36:1-38	☐ 37:1-29	☐ 38:1-31
15	☐ 39:1-43	☐ 40:1-38	☐ Lev 1:1-17	☐ 2:1-16	☐ 3:1-17	☐ 4:1-35	☐ 5:1-19
16	☐ 6:1-30	☐ 7:1-38	☐ 8:1-36	☐ 9:1-24	☐ 10:1-20	☐ 11:1-47	☐ 12:1-8
17	☐ 13:1-28	☐ 13:29-59	☐ 14:1-18	☐ 14:19-32	☐ 14:33-57	☐ 15:1-33	☐ 16:1-17
18	☐ 16:18-34	☐ 17:1-16	☐ 18:1-30	☐ 19:1-37	☐ 20:1-27	☐ 21:1-24	☐ 22:1-33
19	☐ 23:1-22	☐ 23:23-44	☐ 24:1-23	☐ 25:1-23	☐ 25:24-55	☐ 26:1-24	☐ 26:25-46
20	☐ 27:1-34	☐ Num 1:1-54	☐ 2:1-34	☐ 3:1-51	☐ 4:1-49	☐ 5:1-31	☐ 6:1-27
21	☐ 7:1-41	☐ 7:42-88	☐ 7:89—8:26	☐ 9:1-23	☐ 10:1-36	☐ 11:1-35	☐ 12:1—13:33
22	☐ 14:1-45	☐ 15:1-41	☐ 16:1-50	☐ 17:1—18:7	☐ 18:8-32	☐ 19:1-22	☐ 20:1-29
23	☐ 21:1-35	☐ 22:1-41	☐ 23:1-30	☐ 24:1-25	☐ 25:1-18	☐ 26:1-65	☐ 27:1-23
24	☐ 28:1-31	☐ 29:1-40	☐ 30:1—31:24	☐ 31:25-54	☐ 32:1-42	☐ 33:1-56	☐ 34:1-29
25	☐ 35:1-34	☐ 36:1-13	☐ Deut 1:1-46	☐ 2:1-37	☐ 3:1-29	☐ 4:1-49	☐ 5:1-33
26	☐ 6:1—7:26	☐ 8:1-20	☐ 9:1-29	☐ 10:1-22	☐ 11:1-32	☐ 12:1-32	☐ 13:1—14:21

Reading Schedule for the Recovery Version of the Old Testament with Footnotes

Wk.	Lord's Day	Monday	Tuesday	Wednesday	Thursday	Friday	Saturday
27	☐ 14:22—15:23	☐ 16:1-22	☐ 17:1—18:8	☐ 18:9—19:21	☐ 20:1—21:17	☐ 21:18—22:30	☐ 23:1-25
28	☐ 24:1-22	☐ 25:1-19	☐ 26:1-19	☐ 27:1-26	☐ 28:1-68	☐ 29:1-29	☐ 30:1—31:29
29	☐ 31:30—32:52	☐ 33:1-29	☐ 34:1-12	☐ Josh 1:1-18	☐ 2:1-24	☐ 3:1-17	☐ 4:1-24
30	☐ 5:1-15	☐ 6:1-27	☐ 7:1-26	☐ 8:1-35	☐ 9:1-27	☐ 10:1-43	☐ 11:1—12:24
31	☐ 13:1-33	☐ 14:1—15:63	☐ 16:1—18:28	☐ 19:1-51	☐ 20:1—21:45	☐ 22:1-34	☐ 23:1—24:33
32	☐ Judg 1:1-36	☐ 2:1-23	☐ 3:1-31	☐ 4:1-24	☐ 5:1-31	☐ 6:1-40	☐ 7:1-25
33	☐ 8:1-35	☐ 9:1-57	☐ 10:1—11:40	☐ 12:1—13:25	☐ 14:1—15:20	☐ 16:1-31	☐ 17:1—18:31
34	☐ 19:1-30	☐ 20:1-48	☐ 21:1-25	☐ Ruth 1:1-22	☐ 2:1-23	☐ 3:1-18	☐ 4:1-22
35	☐ 1 Sam 1:1-28	☐ 2:1-36	☐ 3:1—4:22	☐ 5:1—6:21	☐ 7:1—8:22	☐ 9:1-27	☐ 10:1—11:15
36	☐ 12:1—13:23	☐ 14:1-52	☐ 15:1-35	☐ 16:1-23	☐ 17:1-58	☐ 18:1-30	☐ 19:1-24
37	☐ 20:1-42	☐ 21:1—22:23	☐ 23:1—24:22	☐ 25:1-44	☐ 26:1-25	☐ 27:1—28:25	☐ 29:1—30:31
38	☐ 31:1-13	☐ 2 Sam 1:1-27	☐ 2:1-32	☐ 3:1-39	☐ 4:1—5:25	☐ 6:1-23	☐ 7:1-29
39	☐ 8:1—9:13	☐ 10:1—11:27	☐ 12:1-31	☐ 13:1-39	☐ 14:1-33	☐ 15:1—16:23	☐ 17:1—18:33
40	☐ 19:1-43	☐ 20:1—21:22	☐ 22:1-51	☐ 23:1-39	☐ 24:1-25	☐ 1 Kings 1:1-19	☐ 1:20-53
41	☐ 2:1-46	☐ 3:1-28	☐ 4:1-34	☐ 5:1—6:38	☐ 7:1-22	☐ 7:23-51	☐ 8:1-36
42	☐ 8:37-66	☐ 9:1-28	☐ 10:1-29	☐ 11:1-43	☐ 12:1-33	☐ 13:1-34	☐ 14:1-31
43	☐ 15:1-34	☐ 16:1—17:24	☐ 18:1-46	☐ 19:1-21	☐ 20:1-43	☐ 21:1—22:53	☐ 2 Kings 1:1-18
44	☐ 2:1—3:27	☐ 4:1-44	☐ 5:1—6:33	☐ 7:1-20	☐ 8:1-29	☐ 9:1-37	☐ 10:1-36
45	☐ 11:1—12:21	☐ 13:1—14:29	☐ 15:1-38	☐ 16:1-20	☐ 17:1-41	☐ 18:1-37	☐ 19:1-37
46	☐ 20:1—21:26	☐ 22:1-20	☐ 23:1-37	☐ 24:1—25:30	☐ 1 Chron 1:1-54	☐ 2:1—3:24	☐ 4:1—5:26
47	☐ 6:1-81	☐ 7:1-40	☐ 8:1-40	☐ 9:1-44	☐ 10:1—11:47	☐ 12:1-40	☐ 13:1—14:17
48	☐ 15:1—16:43	☐ 17:1-27	☐ 18:1—19:19	☐ 20:1—21:30	☐ 22:1—23:32	☐ 24:1—25:31	☐ 26:1-32
49	☐ 27:1-34	☐ 28:1—29:30	☐ 2 Chron 1:1-17	☐ 2:1—3:17	☐ 4:1—5:14	☐ 6:1-42	☐ 7:1—8:18
50	☐ 9:1—10:19	☐ 11:1—12:16	☐ 13:1—15:19	☐ 16:1—17:19	☐ 18:1—19:11	☐ 20:1-37	☐ 21:1—22:12
51	☐ 23:1—24:27	☐ 25:1—26:23	☐ 27:1—28:27	☐ 29:1-36	☐ 30:1—31:21	☐ 32:1-33	☐ 33:1—34:33
52	☐ 35:1—36:23	☐ Ezra 1:1-11	☐ 2:1-70	☐ 3:1—4:24	☐ 5:1—6:22	☐ 7:1-28	☐ 8:1-36

Reading Schedule for the Recovery Version of the Old Testament with Footnotes

Wk.	Lord's Day	Monday	Tuesday	Wednesday	Thursday	Friday	Saturday
53	☐ 9:1—10:44	☐ Neh 1:1-11	☐ 2:1—3:32	☐ 4:1—5:19	☐ 6:1-19	☐ 7:1-73	☐ 8:1-18
54	☐ 9:1-20	☐ 9:21-38	☐ 10:1—11:36	☐ 12:1-47	☐ 13:1-31	☐ Esth 1:1-22	☐ 2:1—3:15
55	☐ 4:1—5:14	☐ 6:1—7:10	☐ 8:1-17	☐ 9:1—10:3	☐ Job 1:1-22	☐ 2:1—3:26	☐ 4:1—5:27
56	☐ 6:1—7:21	☐ 8:1—9:35	☐ 10:1—11:20	☐ 12:1—13:28	☐ 14:1—15:35	☐ 16:1—17:16	☐ 18:1—19:29
57	☐ 20:1—21:34	☐ 22:1—23:17	☐ 24:1—25:6	☐ 26:1—27:23	☐ 28:1—29:25	☐ 30:1—31:40	☐ 32:1—33:33
58	☐ 34:1—35:16	☐ 36:1-33	☐ 37:1-24	☐ 38:1-41	☐ 39:1-30	☐ 40:1-24	☐ 41:1-34
59	☐ 42:1-17	☐ Psa 1:1-6	☐ 2:1—3:8	☐ 4:1—6:10	☐ 7:1—8:9	☐ 9:1—10:18	☐ 11:1—15:5
60	☐ 16:1—17:15	☐ 18:1-50	☐ 19:1—21:13	☐ 22:1-31	☐ 23:1—24:10	☐ 25:1—27:14	☐ 28:1—30:12
61	☐ 31:1—32:11	☐ 33:1—34:22	☐ 35:1—36:12	☐ 37:1-40	☐ 38:1—39:13	☐ 40:1—41:13	☐ 42:1—43:5
62	☐ 44:1-26	☐ 45:1-17	☐ 46:1—48:14	☐ 49:1—50:23	☐ 51:1—52:9	☐ 53:1—55:23	☐ 56:1—58:11
63	☐ 59:1—61:8	☐ 62:1—64:10	☐ 65:1—67:7	☐ 68:1-35	☐ 69:1—70:5	☐ 71:1—72:20	☐ 73:1—74:23
64	☐ 75:1—77:20	☐ 78:1-72	☐ 79:1—81:16	☐ 82:1—84:12	☐ 85:1—87:7	☐ 88:1—89:52	☐ 90:1—91:16
65	☐ 92:1—94:23	☐ 95:1—97:12	☐ 98:1—101:8	☐ 102:1—103:22	☐ 104:1—105:45	☐ 106:1-48	☐ 107:1-43
66	☐ 108:1—109:31	☐ 110:1—112:10	☐ 113:1—115:18	☐ 116:1—118:29	☐ 119:1-32	☐ 119:33-72	☐ 119:73-120
67	☐ 119:121-176	☐ 120:1—124:8	☐ 125:1—128:6	☐ 129:1—132:18	☐ 133:1—135:21	☐ 136:1—138:8	☐ 139:1—140:13
68	☐ 141:1—144:15	☐ 145:1—147:20	☐ 148:1—150:6	☐ Prov 1:1-33	☐ 2:1—3:35	☐ 4:1—5:23	☐ 6:1-35
69	☐ 7:1—8:36	☐ 9:1—10:32	☐ 11:1—12:28	☐ 13:1—14:35	☐ 15:1-33	☐ 16:1-33	☐ 17:1-28
70	☐ 18:1-24	☐ 19:1—20:30	☐ 21:1—22:29	☐ 23:1-35	☐ 24:1—25:28	☐ 26:1—27:27	☐ 28:1—29:27
71	☐ 30:1-33	☐ 31:1-31	☐ Eccl 1:1-18	☐ 2:1—3:22	☐ 4:1—5:20	☐ 6:1—7:29	☐ 8:1—9:18
72	☐ 10:1—11:10	☐ 12:1-14	☐ S.S 1:1-8	☐ 1:9-17	☐ 2:1-17	☐ 3:1-11	☐ 4:1-8
73	☐ 4:9-16	☐ 5:1-16	☐ 6:1-13	☐ 7:1-13	☐ 8:1-14	☐ Isa 1:1-11	☐ 1:12-31
74	☐ 2:1-22	☐ 3:1-26	☐ 4:1-6	☐ 5:1-30	☐ 6:1-13	☐ 7:1-25	☐ 8:1-22
75	☐ 9:1-21	☐ 10:1-34	☐ 11:1—12:6	☐ 13:1-22	☐ 14:1-14	☐ 14:15-32	☐ 15:1—16:14
76	☐ 17:1—18:7	☐ 19:1-25	☐ 20:1—21:17	☐ 22:1-25	☐ 23:1-18	☐ 24:1-23	☐ 25:1-12
77	☐ 26:1-:21	☐ 27:1-13	☐ 28:1-29	☐ 29:1-24	☐ 30:1-33	☐ 31:1—32:20	☐ 33:1-24
78	☐ 34:1-17	☐ 35:1-10	☐ 36:1-22	☐ 37:1-38	☐ 38:1—39:8	☐ 40:1-31	☐ 41:1-29

Reading Schedule for the Recovery Version of the Old Testament with Footnotes

Wk.	Lord's Day	Monday	Tuesday	Wednesday	Thursday	Friday	Saturday
79	42:1-25	43:1-28	44:1-28	45:1-25	46:1-13	47:1-15	48:1-22
80	49:1-13	49:14-26	50:1—51:23	52:1-15	53:1-12	54:1-17	55:1-13
81	56:1-12	57:1-21	58:1-14	59:1-21	60:1-22	61:1-11	62:1-12
82	63:1-19	64:1-12	65:1-25	66:1-24	Jer 1:1-19	2:1-19	2:20-37
83	3:1-25	4:1-31	5:1-31	6:1-30	7:1-34	8:1-22	9:1-26
84	10:1-25	11:1—12:17	13:1-27	14:1-22	15:1-21	16:1—17:27	18:1-23
85	19:1—20:18	21:1—22:30	23:1-40	24:1—25:38	26:1—27:22	28:1—29:32	30:1-24
86	31:1-23	31:24-40	32:1-44	33:1-26	34:1-22	35:1-19	36:1-32
87	37:1-21	38:1-28	39:1—40:16	41:1—42:22	43:1—44:30	45:1—46:28	47:1—48:16
88	48:17-47	49:1-22	49:23-39	50:1-27	50:28-46	51:1-27	51:28-64
89	52:1-34	Lam 1:1-22	2:1-22	3:1-39	3:40-66	4:1-22	5:1-22
90	Ezek 1:1-14	1:15-28	2:1—3:27	4:1—5:17	6:1—7:27	8:1—9:11	10:1—11:25
91	12:1—13:23	14:1—15:8	16:1-63	17:1—18:32	19:1-14	20:1-49	21:1-32
92	22:1-31	23:1-49	24:1-27	25:1—26:21	27:1-36	28:1-26	29:1—30:26
93	31:1—32:32	33:1-33	34:1-31	35:1—36:21	36:22-38	37:1-28	38:1—39:29
94	40:1-27	40:28-49	41:1-26	42:1—43:27	44:1-31	45:1-25	46:1-24
95	47:1-23	48:1-35	Dan 1:1-21	2:1-30	2:31-49	3:1-30	4:1-37
96	5:1-31	6:1-28	7:1-12	7:13-28	8:1-27	9:1-27	10:1-21
97	11:1-22	11:23-45	12:1-13	Hosea 1:1-11	2:1-23	3:1—4:19	5:1-15
98	6:1-11	7:1-16	8:1-14	9:1-17	10:1-15	11:1-12	12:1-14
99	13:1—14:9	Joel 1:1-20	2:1-16	2:17-32	3:1-21	Amos 1:1-15	2:1-16
100	3:1-15	4:1—5:27	6:1—7:17	8:1—9:15	Obad 1-21	Jonah 1:1-17	2:1—4:11
101	Micah 1:1-16	2:1—3:12	4:1—5:15	6:1—7:20	Nahum 1:1-15	2:1—3:19	Hab 1:1-17
102	2:1-20	3:1-19	Zeph 1:1-18	2:1-15	3:1-20	Hag 1:1-15	2:1-23
103	Zech 1:1-21	2:1-13	3:1-10	4:1-14	5:1—6:15	7:1—8:23	9:1-17
104	10:1—11:17	12:1—13:9	14:1-21	Mal 1:1-14	2:1-17	3:1-18	4:1-6

Reading Schedule for the Recovery Version of the New Testament with Footnotes

Wk.	Lord's Day	Monday	Tuesday	Wednesday	Thursday	Friday	Saturday
1	☐ Matt 1:1-2	☐ 1:3-7	☐ 1:8-17	☐ 1:18-25	☐ 2:1-23	☐ 3:1-6	☐ 3:7-17
2	☐ 4:1-11	☐ 4:12-25	☐ 5:1-4	☐ 5:5-12	☐ 5:13-20	☐ 5:21-26	☐ 5:27-48
3	☐ 6:1-8	☐ 6:9-18	☐ 6:19-34	☐ 7:1-12	☐ 7:13-29	☐ 8:1-13	☐ 8:14-22
4	☐ 8:23-34	☐ 9:1-13	☐ 9:14-17	☐ 9:18-34	☐ 9:35—10:5	☐ 10:6-25	☐ 10:26-42
5	☐ 11:1-15	☐ 11:16-30	☐ 12:1-14	☐ 12:15-32	☐ 12:33-42	☐ 12:43—13:2	☐ 13:3-12
6	☐ 13:13-30	☐ 13:31-43	☐ 13:44-58	☐ 14:1-13	☐ 14:14-21	☐ 14:22-36	☐ 15:1-20
7	☐ 15:21-31	☐ 15:32-39	☐ 16:1-12	☐ 16:13-20	☐ 16:21-28	☐ 17:1-13	☐ 17:14-27
8	☐ 18:1-14	☐ 18:15-22	☐ 18:23-35	☐ 19:1-15	☐ 19:16-30	☐ 20:1-16	☐ 20:17-34
9	☐ 21:1-11	☐ 21:12-22	☐ 21:23-32	☐ 21:33-46	☐ 22:1-22	☐ 22:23-33	☐ 22:34-46
10	☐ 23:1-12	☐ 23:13-39	☐ 24:1-14	☐ 24:15-31	☐ 24:32-51	☐ 25:1-13	☐ 25:14-30
11	☐ 25:31-46	☐ 26:1-16	☐ 26:17-35	☐ 26:36-46	☐ 26:47-64	☐ 26:65-75	☐ 27:1-26
12	☐ 27:27-44	☐ 27:45-56	☐ 27:57—28:15	☐ 28:16-20	☐ Mark 1:1	☐ 1:2-6	☐ 1:7-13
13	☐ 1:14-28	☐ 1:29-45	☐ 2:1-12	☐ 2:13-28	☐ 3:1-19	☐ 3:20-35	☐ 4:1-25
14	☐ 4:26-41	☐ 5:1-20	☐ 5:21-43	☐ 6:1-29	☐ 6:30-56	☐ 7:1-23	☐ 7:24-37
15	☐ 8:1-26	☐ 8:27—9:1	☐ 9:2-29	☐ 9:30-50	☐ 10:1-16	☐ 10:17-34	☐ 10:35-52
16	☐ 11:1-16	☐ 11:17-33	☐ 12:1-27	☐ 12:28-44	☐ 13:1-13	☐ 13:14-37	☐ 14:1-26
17	☐ 14:27-52	☐ 14:53-72	☐ 15:1-15	☐ 15:16-47	☐ 16:1-8	☐ 16:9-20	☐ Luke 1:1-4
18	☐ 1:5-25	☐ 1:26-46	☐ 1:47-56	☐ 1:57-80	☐ 2:1-8	☐ 2:9-20	☐ 2:21-39
19	☐ 2:40-52	☐ 3:1-20	☐ 3:21-38	☐ 4:1-13	☐ 4:14-30	☐ 4:31-44	☐ 5:1-26
20	☐ 5:27—6:16	☐ 6:17-38	☐ 6:39-49	☐ 7:1-17	☐ 7:18-23	☐ 7:24-35	☐ 7:36-50
21	☐ 8:1-15	☐ 8:16-25	☐ 8:26-39	☐ 8:40-56	☐ 9:1-17	☐ 9:18-26	☐ 9:27-36
22	☐ 9:37-50	☐ 9:51-62	☐ 10:1-11	☐ 10:12-24	☐ 10:25-37	☐ 10:38-42	☐ 11:1-13
23	☐ 11:14-26	☐ 11:27-36	☐ 11:37-54	☐ 12:1-12	☐ 12:13-21	☐ 12:22-34	☐ 12:35-48
24	☐ 12:49-59	☐ 13:1-9	☐ 13:10-17	☐ 13:18-30	☐ 13:31—14:6	☐ 14:7-14	☐ 14:15-24
25	☐ 14:25-35	☐ 15:1-10	☐ 15:11-21	☐ 15:22-32	☐ 16:1-13	☐ 16:14-22	☐ 16:23-31
26	☐ 17:1-19	☐ 17:20-37	☐ 18:1-14	☐ 18:15-30	☐ 18:31-43	☐ 19:1-10	☐ 19:11-27

Reading Schedule for the Recovery Version of the New Testament with Footnotes

Wk.	Lord's Day	Monday	Tuesday	Wednesday	Thursday	Friday	Saturday
27	☐ Luke 19:28-48	☐ 20:1-19	☐ 20:20-38	☐ 20:39—21:4	☐ 21:5-27	☐ 21:28-38	☐ 22:1-20
28	☐ 22:21-38	☐ 22:39-54	☐ 22:55-71	☐ 23:1-43	☐ 23:44-56	☐ 24:1-12	☐ 24:13-35
29	☐ 24:36-53	☐ John 1:1-13	☐ 1:14-18	☐ 1:19-34	☐ 1:35-51	☐ 2:1-11	☐ 2:12-22
30	☐ 2:23—3:13	☐ 3:14-21	☐ 3:22-36	☐ 4:1-14	☐ 4:15-26	☐ 4:27-42	☐ 4:43-54
31	☐ 5:1-16	☐ 5:17-30	☐ 5:31-47	☐ 6:1-15	☐ 6:16-31	☐ 6:32-51	☐ 6:52-71
32	☐ 7:1-9	☐ 7:10-24	☐ 7:25-36	☐ 7:37-52	☐ 7:53—8:11	☐ 8:12-27	☐ 8:28-44
33	☐ 8:45-59	☐ 9:1-13	☐ 9:14-34	☐ 9:35—10:9	☐ 10:10-30	☐ 10:31—11:4	☐ 11:5-22
34	☐ 11:23-40	☐ 11:41-57	☐ 12:1-11	☐ 12:12-24	☐ 12:25-36	☐ 12:37-50	☐ 13:1-11
35	☐ 13:12-30	☐ 13:31-38	☐ 14:1-6	☐ 14:7-20	☐ 14:21-31	☐ 15:1-11	☐ 15:12-27
36	☐ 16:1-15	☐ 16:16-33	☐ 17:1-5	☐ 17:6-13	☐ 17:14-24	☐ 17:25—18:11	☐ 18:12-27
37	☐ 18:28-40	☐ 19:1-16	☐ 19:17-30	☐ 19:31-42	☐ 20:1-13	☐ 20:14-18	☐ 20:19-22
38	☐ 20:23-31	☐ 21:1-14	☐ 21:15-22	☐ 21:23-25	☐ Acts 1:1-8	☐ 1:9-14	☐ 1:15-26
39	☐ 2:1-13	☐ 2:14-21	☐ 2:22-36	☐ 2:37-41	☐ 2:42-47	☐ 3:1-18	☐ 3:19—4:22
40	☐ 4:23-37	☐ 5:1-16	☐ 5:17-32	☐ 5:33-42	☐ 6:1—7:1	☐ 7:2-29	☐ 7:30-60
41	☐ 8:1-13	☐ 8:14-25	☐ 8:26-40	☐ 9:1-19	☐ 9:20-43	☐ 10:1-16	☐ 10:17-33
42	☐ 10:34-48	☐ 11:1-18	☐ 11:19-30	☐ 12:1-25	☐ 13:1-12	☐ 13:13-43	☐ 13:44—14:5
43	☐ 14:6-28	☐ 15:1-12	☐ 15:13-34	☐ 15:35—16:5	☐ 16:6-18	☐ 16:19-40	☐ 17:1-18
44	☐ 17:19-34	☐ 18:1-17	☐ 18:18-28	☐ 19:1-20	☐ 19:21-41	☐ 20:1-12	☐ 20:13-38
45	☐ 21:1-14	☐ 21:15-26	☐ 21:27-40	☐ 22:1-21	☐ 22:22-29	☐ 22:30—23:11	☐ 23:12-15
46	☐ 23:16-30	☐ 23:31—24:21	☐ 24:22—25:5	☐ 25:6-27	☐ 26:1-13	☐ 26:14-32	☐ 27:1-26
47	☐ 27:27—28:10	☐ 28:11-22	☐ 28:23-31	☐ Rom 1:1-2	☐ 1:3-7	☐ 1:8-17	☐ 1:18-25
48	☐ 1:26—2:10	☐ 2:11-29	☐ 3:1-20	☐ 3:21-31	☐ 4:1-12	☐ 4:13-25	☐ 5:1-11
49	☐ 5:12-17	☐ 5:18—6:5	☐ 6:6-11	☐ 6:12-23	☐ 7:1-12	☐ 7:13-25	☐ 8:1-2
50	☐ 8:3-6	☐ 8:7-13	☐ 8:14-25	☐ 8:26-39	☐ 9:1-18	☐ 9:19—10:3	☐ 10:4-15
51	☐ 10:16—11:10	☐ 11:11-22	☐ 11:23-36	☐ 12:1-3	☐ 12:4-21	☐ 13:1-14	☐ 14:1-12
52	☐ 14:13-23	☐ 15:1-13	☐ 15:14-33	☐ 16:1-5	☐ 16:6-24	☐ 16:25-27	☐ 1 Cor 1:1-4

Reading Schedule for the Recovery Version of the New Testament with Footnotes

Wk.	Lord's Day	Monday	Tuesday	Wednesday	Thursday	Friday	Saturday
53	☐ 1 Cor 1:5-9	☐ 1:10-17	☐ 1:18-31	☐ 2:1-5	☐ 2:6-10	☐ 2:11-16	☐ 3:1-9
54	☐ 3:10-13	☐ 3:14-23	☐ 4:1-9	☐ 4:10-21	☐ 5:1-13	☐ 6:1-11	☐ 6:12-20
55	☐ 7:1-16	☐ 7:17-24	☐ 7:25-40	☐ 8:1-13	☐ 9:1-15	☐ 9:16-27	☐ 10:1-4
56	☐ 10:5-13	☐ 10:14-33	☐ 11:1-6	☐ 11:7-16	☐ 11:17-26	☐ 11:27-34	☐ 12:1-11
57	☐ 12:12-22	☐ 12:23-31	☐ 13:1-13	☐ 14:1-12	☐ 14:13-25	☐ 14:26-33	☐ 14:34-40
58	☐ 15:1-19	☐ 15:20-28	☐ 15:29-34	☐ 15:35-49	☐ 15:50-58	☐ 16:1-9	☐ 16:10-24
59	☐ 2 Cor 1:1-4	☐ 1:5-14	☐ 1:15-22	☐ 1:23—2:11	☐ 2:12-17	☐ 3:1-6	☐ 3:7-11
60	☐ 3:12-18	☐ 4:1-6	☐ 4:7-12	☐ 4:13-18	☐ 5:1-8	☐ 5:9-15	☐ 5:16-21
61	☐ 6:1-13	☐ 6:14—7:4	☐ 7:5-16	☐ 8:1-15	☐ 8:16-24	☐ 9:1-15	☐ 10:1-6
62	☐ 10:7-18	☐ 11:1-15	☐ 11:16-33	☐ 12:1-10	☐ 12:11-21	☐ 13:1-10	☐ 13:11-14
63	☐ Gal 1:1-5	☐ 1:6-14	☐ 1:15-24	☐ 2:1-13	☐ 2:14-21	☐ 3:1-4	☐ 3:5-14
64	☐ 3:15-22	☐ 3:23-29	☐ 4:1-7	☐ 4:8-20	☐ 4:21-31	☐ 5:1-12	☐ 5:13-21
65	☐ 5:22-26	☐ 6:1-10	☐ 6:11-15	☐ 6:16-18	☐ Eph 1:1-3	☐ 1:4-6	☐ 1:7-10
66	☐ 1:11-14	☐ 1:15-18	☐ 1:19-23	☐ 2:1-5	☐ 2:6-10	☐ 2:11-14	☐ 2:15-18
67	☐ 2:19-22	☐ 3:1-7	☐ 3:8-13	☐ 3:14-18	☐ 3:19-21	☐ 4:1-4	☐ 4:5-10
68	☐ 4:11-16	☐ 4:17-24	☐ 4:25-32	☐ 5:1-10	☐ 5:11-21	☐ 5:22-26	☐ 5:27-33
69	☐ 6:1-9	☐ 6:10-14	☐ 6:15-18	☐ 6:19-24	☐ Phil 1:1-7	☐ 1:8-18	☐ 1:19-26
70	☐ 1:27—2:4	☐ 2:5-11	☐ 2:12-16	☐ 2:17-30	☐ 3:1-6`	☐ 3:7-11	☐ 3:12-16
71	☐ 3:17-21	☐ 4:1-9	☐ 4:10-23	☐ Col 1:1-8	☐ 1:9-13	☐ 1:14-23	☐ 1:24-29
72	☐ 2:1-7	☐ 2:8-15	☐ 2:16-23	☐ 3:1-4	☐ 3:5-15	☐ 3:16-25	☐ 4:1-18
73	☐ 1 Thes 1:1-3	☐ 1:4-10	☐ 2:1-12	☐ 2:13—3:5	☐ 3:6-13	☐ 4:1-10	☐ 4:11—5:11
74	☐ 5:12-28	☐ 2 Thes 1:1-12	☐ 2:1-17	☐ 3:1-18	☐ 1 Tim 1:1-2	☐ 1:3-4	☐ 1:5-14
75	☐ 1:15-20	☐ 2:1-7	☐ 2:8-15	☐ 3:1-13	☐ 3:14—4:5	☐ 4:6-16	☐ 5:1-25
76	☐ 6:1-10	☐ 6:11-21	☐ 2 Tim 1:1-10	☐ 1:11-18	☐ 2:1-15	☐ 2:16-26	☐ 3:1-13
77	☐ 3:14—4:8	☐ 4:9-22	☐ Titus 1:1-4	☐ 1:5-16	☐ 2:1-15	☐ 3:1-8	☐ 3:9-15
78	☐ Philem 1:1-11	☐ 1:12-25	☐ Heb 1:1-2	☐ 1:3-5	☐ 1:6-14	☐ 2:1-9	☐ 2:10-18

Reading Schedule for the Recovery Version of the New Testament with Footnotes

Wk.	Lord's Day	Monday	Tuesday	Wednesday	Thursday	Friday	Saturday
79	☐ Heb 3:1-6	☐ 3:7-19	☐ 4:1-9	☐ 4:10-13	☐ 4:14-16	☐ 5:1-10	☐ 5:11—6:3
80	☐ 6:4-8	☐ 6:9-20	☐ 7:1-10	☐ 7:11-28	☐ 8:1-6	☐ 8:7-13	☐ 9:1-4
81	☐ 9:5-14	☐ 9:15-28	☐ 10:1-18	☐ 10:19-28	☐ 10:29-39	☐ 11:1-6	☐ 11:7-19
82	☐ 11:20-31	☐ 11:32-40	☐ 12:1-2	☐ 12:3-13	☐ 12:14-17	☐ 12:18-26	☐ 12:27-29
83	☐ 13:1-7	☐ 13:8-12	☐ 13:13-15	☐ 13:16-25	☐ James 1:1-8	☐ 1:9-18	☐ 1:19-27
84	☐ 2:1-13	☐ 2:14-26	☐ 3:1-18	☐ 4:1-10	☐ 4:11-17	☐ 5:1-12	☐ 5:13-20
85	☐ 1 Pet 1:1-2	☐ 1:3-4	☐ 1:5	☐ 1:6-9	☐ 1:10-12	☐ 1:13-17	☐ 1:18-25
86	☐ 2:1-3	☐ 2:4-8	☐ 2:9-17	☐ 2:18-25	☐ 3:1-13	☐ 3:14-22	☐ 4:1-6
87	☐ 4:7-16	☐ 4:17-19	☐ 5:1-4	☐ 5:5-9	☐ 5:10-14	☐ 2 Pet 1:1-2	☐ 1:3-4
88	☐ 1:5-8	☐ 1:9-11	☐ 1:12-18	☐ 1:19-21	☐ 2:1-3	☐ 2:4-11	☐ 2:12-22
89	☐ 3:1-6	☐ 3:7-9	☐ 3:10-12	☐ 3:13-15	☐ 3:16	☐ 3:17-18	☐ 1 John 1:1-2
90	☐ 1:3-4	☐ 1:5	☐ 1:6	☐ 1:7	☐ 1:8-10	☐ 2:1-2	☐ 2:3-11
91	☐ 2:12-14	☐ 2:15-19	☐ 2:20-23	☐ 2:24-27	☐ 2:28-29	☐ 3:1-5	☐ 3:6-10
92	☐ 3:11-18	☐ 3:19-24	☐ 4:1-6	☐ 4:7-11	☐ 4:12-15	☐ 4:16—5:3	☐ 5:4-13
93	☐ 5:14-17	☐ 5:18-21	☐ 2 John 1:1-3	☐ 1:4-9	☐ 1:10-13	☐ 3 John 1:1-6	☐ 1:7-14
94	☐ Jude 1:1-4	☐ 1:5-10	☐ 1:11-19	☐ 1:20-25	☐ Rev 1:1-3	☐ 1:4-6	☐ 1:7-11
95	☐ 1:12-13	☐ 1:14-16	☐ 1:17-20	☐ 2:1-6	☐ 2:7	☐ 2:8-9	☐ 2:10-11
96	☐ 2:12-14	☐ 2:15-17	☐ 2:18-23	☐ 2:24-29	☐ 3:1-3	☐ 3:4-6	☐ 3:7-9
97	☐ 3:10-13	☐ 3:14-18	☐ 3:19-22	☐ 4:1-5	☐ 4:6-7	☐ 4:8-11	☐ 5:1-6
98	☐ 5:7-14	☐ 6:1-8	☐ 6:9-17	☐ 7:1-8	☐ 7:9-17	☐ 8:1-6	☐ 8:7-12
99	☐ 8:13—9:11	☐ 9:12-21	☐ 10:1-4	☐ 10:5-11	☐ 11:1-4	☐ 11:5-14	☐ 11:15-19
100	☐ 12:1-4	☐ 12:5-9	☐ 12:10-18	☐ 13:1-10	☐ 13:11-18	☐ 14:1-5	☐ 14:6-12
101	☐ 14:13-20	☐ 15:1-8	☐ 16:1-12	☐ 16:13-21	☐ 17:1-6	☐ 17:7-18	☐ 18:1-8
102	☐ 18:9—19:4	☐ 19:5-10	☐ 19:11-16	☐ 19:17-21	☐ 20:1-6	☐ 20:7-10	☐ 20:11-15
103	☐ 21:1	☐ 21:2	☐ 21:3-8	☐ 21:9-13	☐ 21:14-18	☐ 21:19-21	☐ 21:22-27
104	☐ 22:1	☐ 22:2	☐ 22:3-11	☐ 22:12-15	☐ 22:16-17	☐ 22:18-21	☐

Week 1 — Day 6 — Today's verses

Mark 9:31 For He was teaching His disciples. And He said to them, The Son of Man is being delivered into the hands of men, and they will kill Him; and when He has been killed, after three days He will rise.

Mark 16:19-20 So then the Lord Jesus, after speaking to them, was taken up into heaven and sat at the right hand of God. And they went out and preached everywhere, the Lord working with *them* and confirming the word by the accompanying signs.

Date

Week 1 — Day 3 — Today's verses

Mark 6:45-48 And immediately He compelled His disciples to step into the boat and go before to the other side....And... He went away to the mountain to pray. And when evening fell,...He was alone on the land. And seeing them distressed as they rowed, for the wind was contrary to them, He came toward them about the fourth watch of the night, walking on the sea....

51 And He went up unto them into the boat, and the wind ceased....

Date

Week 1 — Day 5 — Today's verses

Mark 1:30-31 ...Simon's mother-in-law was lying down with a fever, ...and He came to *her* and raised her up, holding her hand, and the fever left her....

42 And...the leprosy left him, and he was cleansed.

2:10-11 ...He said to the paralytic, to you I say, Rise, take up your mat and go to your house.

5:29 ...Immediately the fountain of her blood was dried up...

Date

Week 1 — Day 2 — Today's verses

Mark 16:7 But go, tell His disciples and Peter that He is going before you into Galilee. There you will see Him, even as He told you.

Date

Week 1 — Day 4 — Today's verses

Mark 1:15 And saying, The time is fulfilled and the kingdom of God has drawn near. Repent and believe in the gospel.

Date

Week 1 — Day 1 — Today's verses

Eph. 4:22-24 That you put off, as regards your former manner of life, the old man, which is being corrupted,...and *that* you be renewed in the spirit of your mind and put on the new man, which was created according to God...

Mark 8:34 ...He called the crowd to *Him* with His disciples and said to them, If anyone wants to follow after Me, let him deny himself and take up his cross and follow Me.

1 Pet. 2:21 For to this you were called, because Christ also suffered on your behalf, leaving you a model so that you may follow in His steps.

Date

Week 2 — Day 1 — Today's verses

Mark And whoever wants to be first among you
10:44-45 shall be the slave of all. For even the Son of Man did not come to be served, but to serve and to give His life as a ransom for many.

Rom. Paul, a slave of Christ Jesus, a called apos-
1:1 tle, separated unto the gospel of God.

Date

Week 2 — Day 2 — Today's verses

Phil. But emptied Himself, taking the form of a
2:7-9 slave, becoming in the likeness of men; and being found in fashion as a man, He humbled Himself, becoming obedient even unto death, and *that* the death of a cross. Therefore also God highly exalted Him and bestowed on Him the name which is above every name.

Date

Week 2 — Day 3 — Today's verses

Phil. For God is my witness how I long after
1:8 you all in the inward parts of Christ Jesus.
2:5-6 Let this mind be in you, which was also in Christ Jesus, who, existing in the form of God, did not consider being equal with God a treasure to be grasped.

Date

Week 2 — Day 4 — Today's verses

Isa. He will not cry out, nor lift up His voice, /
42:2 Nor make His voice heard in the street.
3 A bruised reed He will not break; / And a dimly burning flax He will not extinguish; / He will bring forth justice in truth.
4 He will not faint, nor will He be discouraged....
50:4 The Lord Jehovah has given me / The tongue of the instructed, / That I should know how to sustain the weary with a word. / He awakens me morning by morning; / He awakens my ear / To hear as an instructed one.

Date

Week 2 — Day 5 — Today's verses

Exo. But if the servant plainly says, I love my
21:5-6 master, my wife, and my children; I will not go out free; then his master shall bring him to God and shall bring him to the door or to the doorpost, and his master shall bore his ear through with an awl; and he shall serve him forever.

Eph. And walk in love, even as Christ also
5:2 loved us and gave Himself up for us, an offering and a sacrifice to God for a sweet-smelling savor.

Date

Week 2 — Day 6 — Today's verses

Mark And Jesus called them to *Him* and said to
10:42-43 them, You know that those who are esteemed as rulers of the Gentiles lord it over them, and their great ones exercise authority over them. But it is not so among you; but whoever wants to become great among you shall be your servant.

2 Cor. But I, I will most gladly spend and be ut-
12:15 terly spent on behalf of your souls....

Date

Week 3 — Day 1

Today's verses

Luke
22:26-27
But you shall not be so; but let the greatest among you become like the youngest, and the one who leads like the one who serves. For who is greater, the one who reclines at table or the one who serves? Is it not the one who reclines at table? But I am in your midst as the one who serves.

Luke
12:37
Blessed are those slaves whom the master, when he comes, will find watching. Truly I tell you that he will gird himself and will have them recline at table, and he will come to them and serve them.

Date _____

Week 3 — Day 2

Today's verses

Mark
1:14-15
And after John was delivered up, Jesus came into Galilee, proclaiming the gospel of God, and saying, The time is fulfilled, and the kingdom of God has drawn near. Repent and believe in the gospel.

38
And He said to them, Let us go elsewhere into the nearby towns that I may preach there also, because for this *purpose* I came out.

Date _____

Week 3 — Day 3

Today's verses

Mark
1:21-22
...And immediately, on the Sabbath, He entered into the synagogue and taught. And they were astounded at His teaching, for He taught them as One having authority and not like the scribes.

John
8:32, 36
And you shall know the truth, and the truth shall set you free....If therefore the Son sets you free, you shall be free indeed.

Date _____

Week 3 — Day 4

Today's verses

Mark
1:34-35
And He healed many who were ill with various diseases, and He cast out many demons and did not allow the demons to speak, because they knew Him. And rising very early in the morning, *while it was still* night, He went out and went away to a deserted place, and there He prayed.

1 John
3:8
...For this purpose the Son of God was manifested, that He might destroy the works of the devil.

Date _____

Week 3 — Day 5

Today's verses

Mark
1:40-42
And a leper came to Him, entreating Him and falling on his knees and saying to Him, If You are willing, You can cleanse me. And He was moved with compassion, and stretching out His hand, He touched him and said to him, I am willing; be cleansed! And immediately the leprosy left him, and he was cleansed.

Date _____

Week 3 — Day 6

Today's verses

Lev.
14:34-35
When you come into the land of Canaan, which I give you for a possession, and I put the infection of leprosy in a house in the land of your possession, then he to whom the house belongs shall come and tell the priest, saying, It seems to me that *there is* something like an infection in the house.

Heb.
9:14
How much more will the blood of Christ, who through the eternal Spirit offered Himself without blemish to God, purify our conscience from dead works to serve the living God?

Date _____

Week 4 — Day 1

Today's verses

Mark 2:5 And Jesus, seeing their faith, said to the paralytic, Child, your sins are forgiven.

8-11 And immediately Jesus, knowing fully in His spirit that they were reasoning this way within themselves, said to them, Why are you reasoning about these things in your hearts? Which is easier: to say to the paralytic, Your sins are forgiven, or to say, Rise and take up your mat and walk? But that you may know that the Son of Man has authority to forgive sins on earth—He said to the paralytic, To you I say, Rise, take up your mat and go to your house.

_____
Date

Week 4 — Day 2

Today's verses

Mark 2:15-17 And as He reclined *at table* in his house, many tax collectors and sinners were reclining together with Jesus and His disciples, for there were many, and they were following Him. And the scribes of the Pharisees, seeing that He ate with sinners and tax collectors, said to His disciples, Why does He eat with tax collectors and sinners? And when Jesus heard *this*, He said to them, Those who are strong have no need of a physician, but those who are ill; I did not come to call the righteous, but sinners.

_____
Date

Week 4 — Day 3

Today's verses

Mark 2:18-19 ...Why do the disciples of John and the disciples of the Pharisees fast, but Your disciples do not fast? And Jesus said to them, The sons of the bridechamber cannot fast while the bridegroom is with them, can they? For as long a time as they have the bridegroom with them they cannot fast.

21-22 No one sews a patch of unfulled cloth on an old garment; otherwise, that which fills it up pulls away from it, the new from the old, and a worse tear is made. And no one puts new wine into old wineskins; otherwise, the wine will burst the wineskins, and the wine is ruined as well as the wineskins; but new wine *is put* into fresh wineskins.

_____
Date

Week 4 — Day 4

Today's verses

Mark 2:25-28 And He said to them, Have you never read what David did when he had need and became hungry, he and those with him; how he entered into the house of God during the time of Abiathar the high priest and ate the bread of the Presence, which is not lawful *for anyone* to eat except the priests, and he gave also to those who were with him? And He said to them, The Sabbath came into being for man, and not man for the Sabbath. So then the Son of Man is Lord even of the Sabbath.

_____
Date

Week 4 — Day 5

Today's verses

Mark 3:2-5 And they were watching Him closely *to see* if He would heal him on the Sabbath, so that they might accuse Him. And He said to the man who had the withered hand, Rise *and stand* in the midst. And He said to them, Is it lawful on the Sabbath to do good or to do evil, to save life or to kill? But they remained silent. And looking around at them with anger and being greatly grieved with the hardness of their heart, He said to the man, Stretch out your hand. And he stretched *it* out, and his hand was restored.

_____
Date

Week 4 — Day 6

Today's verses

Mark 5:27-29 When she heard the things concerning Jesus, she came up in the crowd behind *Him* and touched His garment, for she said, If I touch even His garments, I will be healed. And immediately the fountain of her blood was dried up, and she knew in her body that she was cured of the affliction.

34 And He said to her, Daughter, your faith has healed you. Go in peace and be well from your affliction.

_____
Date

Week 5 — Day 6   Today's verses

Rom. For the mind set on the flesh is death, but
8:6 the mind set on the spirit is life and peace.

Col. When Christ our life is manifested, then
3:4 you also will be manifested with Him in glory.

Phil. For to me, to live is Christ and to die is
1:21 gain.

Date

Week 5 — Day 5   Today's verses

1 Cor. But of Him you are in Christ Jesus, who
1:30 became wisdom to us from God: both righteousness and sanctification and redemption.

Gal. I am crucified with Christ; and *it is* no lon-
2:20 ger I *who* live, but *it is* Christ *who* lives in me; and the *life* which I now live in the flesh I live in faith, the *faith* of the Son of God, who loved me and gave Himself up for me.

Date

Week 5 — Day 4   Today's verses

Mark So then the Lord Jesus, after speaking to
16:19-20 them, was taken up into heaven and sat at the right hand of God. And they went out and preached everywhere, the Lord working with *them* and confirming the word by the accompanying signs.

Date

Week 5 — Day 3   Today's verses

Mark And immediately the Spirit thrust Him out
1:12-13 into the wilderness. And He was in the wilderness forty days, being tempted by Satan; and He was with the wild animals, and the angels ministered to Him.

Date

Week 5 — Day 2   Today's verses

Mark I have baptized you in water, but He Him-
1:8 self will baptize you in the Holy Spirit.

Matt. Then Jesus came from Galilee to the Jor-
3:13-15 dan to John to be baptized by him. But John tried to prevent Him, saying, *It is* I *who* have need of being baptized by You, and You come to me? But Jesus answered and said to him, Permit it for now, for it is fitting for us in this way to fulfill all righteousness. Then he permitted Him.

Date

Week 5 — Day 1   Today's verses

Mark The beginning of the gospel of Jesus Christ,
1:1-6 the Son of God, even as it is written in Isaiah the prophet: "Behold, I send My messenger before Your face, who will prepare Your way, a voice of one crying in the wilderness: Prepare the way of the Lord; make straight His paths." John came baptizing in the wilderness and preaching a baptism of repentance for forgiveness of sins. And all the *region* of Judea went out to him, and all the *people* of Jerusalem; and they were baptized by him in the Jordan River, as they confessed their sins. And John was clothed in camel's hair and *had* a leather girdle around his loins, and he ate locusts and wild honey.

Date

Week 6 — Day 4 Today's verses

Mark And other *seed* fell into the thorns, and
4:7 the thorns came up and utterly choked it,
and it yielded no fruit.

18-19 And others are the ones being sown into
the thorns; these are the ones who have
heard the word, and the anxieties of the
age and the deceitfulness of riches and
the lusts for other things enter in and utterly choke the word, and it becomes unfruitful.

1 Tim. But godliness with contentment is great
6:6 gain.

_____
Date

Week 6 — Day 5 Today's verses

Mark And others fell into the good earth and
4:8 yielded fruit, coming up and growing;
and one bore thirtyfold, and one
sixtyfold, and one a hundredfold.

20 And these are the ones sown on the good
earth: *those* who hear the word and receive *it* and bear fruit, one thirtyfold, and
one sixtyfold, and one a hundredfold.

_____
Date

Week 6 — Day 6 Today's verses

Mark ...The kingdom of God has drawn near.
1:15 Repent and believe in the gospel.

_____
Date

Week 6 — Day 1 Today's verses

Mark Listen! Behold, the sower went out to
4:3 sow.

14 The sower sows the word.

26 And He said, So is the kingdom of God: as
if a man cast seed on the earth.

_____
Date

Week 6 — Day 2 Today's verses

Mark And as he sowed, some *seed* fell beside
4:4 the way, and the birds came and devoured it.

15 ...These are...beside the way, where the
word is sown; and when they hear, immediately Satan comes and takes away the
word which has been sown into them.

_____
Date

Week 6 — Day 3 Today's verses

Mark And other *seed* fell on the rocky place,
4:5-6 where it did not have much earth, and immediately it sprang up because it had no
depth of earth. And when the sun rose, it
was scorched; and because it had no root,
it withered.

16-17 And likewise, these are the ones being
sown on the rocky places, who, when
they hear the word, immediately receive
it with joy. Yet they have no root in themselves, but last only for a time; then when
affliction or persecution occurs because
of the word, immediately they are
stumbled.

_____
Date